The Best  g

BRIDGE FROM VIRGINIA ST.

W H E E L I N G

Wheeling Suspension Bridge

Located at 10th and Main streets, the Wheeling Suspension Bridge is the most important pre-Civil War structure in the country. The bridge was designed by Charles Ellet, Jr. and was dedicated on November 15, 1849. In celebration of the opening of the bridge, it was illuminated with 1,010 lights, one light for each foot of the bridge's length. The method of illumination remains a mystery.

At completion, it was the longest bridge in the world, and the first to cross the almost 1,000-mile-long Ohio River.

On May 17, 1854, the suspension bridge blew down in a windstorm. Ellet rebuilt the bridge in forty days. He salvaged the cables from the bottom of the Ohio River and made the deck a single lane, necessitating one-way traffic. The bridge was returned to its original width in 1860. It was strengthened and stiffened with stay cables in 1871–72 using the plan of Washington Roebling, son of John Roebling, famous for the design of the Brooklyn Bridge.

The Wheeling Suspension Bridge has been designated a National Civil Engineering Landmark, as well as a National Historic Landmark. The bridge is still used by locals, and remains a favorite vantage point for viewing the Fourth of July fireworks.

Photograph courtesy of Gary Zearott, Zee Photo, photo date 1886

This cookbook is a collection of favorite recipes, which are not necessarily original recipes.

Published by: The Junior League of Wheeling, Inc.

Copyright© The Junior League of Wheeling, Inc.
907½ National Road, Wheeling, West Virginia 26003
1-304-232-3164

Library of Congress Number: 94-71854
ISBN: 0-87197-404-5

Designed, Edited and Printed by: Favorite Recipes® Press
P.O. Box 305142, Nashville, Tennessee 37230
1-800-358-0560

Manufactured in the United States of America
First Printing: 1994   10,000 copies
Second Printing: 1997   4,000 copies

Cookbook Committee

Wendy Fluty Hinerman, Chairman
Jo Ellen M. Miller, Co-Chairman

Stephanie W. Grove	Appetizers and Beverages
Jan Heslep Berardinelli	Soups and Sandwiches
	Salads
Caryn H. Buch	Entrées
Gay B. Kramer	Vegetables and Side Dishes
Judi Young Tarowsky	Pasta
Samantha Hensel Buch	Bread and Breakfast
Brenda G. Moore	Cookies and Candy
	Desserts
Kathy Parsons	Recipe Coordinator
Janie Altmeyer	Chocolate Advisor

Proofreading Committee
Janie Altmeyer, Jan Berardinelli, Caryn Buch, Samantha Buch,
Cheryl Danehart, Beverly B. Fluty, Stephanie Grove,
Wendy Hinerman, Gay Kramer, Jo Ellen Miller, Kathy Parsons,
Kathy Tannenbaum, Judi Tarowsky

Local History Advisor: Beverly B. Fluty

Drawings by: Susan Miller

Cover artwork reproduced from original painting by Don Fusco

Grateful acknowledgements to Scott, Ted, and Rob
and all of our long-suffering husbands.

♥ Hugs and kisses to our children who taste-tested recipes. ♥

JLW, Inc.

The Association of Junior Leagues International, Inc. is a thriving organization of 190,000 members in 285 Junior Leagues in the United States, Canada, Mexico, and Great Britain. It was established in 1901 by Mary Harriman of New York City.

The Junior League of Wheeling, Inc. started as a service league with sixty-nine young women in 1931. We became a member of the Association of Junior Leagues of America in 1940.

We are an organization of women committed to promoting voluntarism and to improving the community through the effective action and leadership of trained volunteers. The purpose of the JLW, Inc. is exclusively educational and charitable.

The proceeds from the sale of this cookbook will be used in our community to create a positive impact. We appreciate your support for this project.

Architectural Directory

 Detail from front entrance way, 921 Main Street

 Terra Cotta Detail, 1201 Main Street

 Cockscomb detail on iron fence, 2307 Chapline Street

 Detail from cast-iron window box, 811 Main Street

 Detail on gate, adjacent to 57 Fourteenth Street

 Entrance fanlight window, Fourteenth and Chapline Street

 Detail from stained glass window, Stifel Fine Arts Center

 Animal medallion, Centre Market House

 Stone embellishment above stained glass window, 2319 Chapline Street

 Monument, Greenwood Cemetery

 Detail from mantle, Stifel Fine Arts Center

 Stained glass window, 325 North Front Street

 Swag decoration on oriel, 59 Fourteenth Street

 Lyre in medallion, 1015 Main Street

 Ivy detail on iron fence, 827 Main Street

Contents

Contents

Introduction

In 1749, a French expedition buried a leaden plate at the confluence of Wheeling Creek and the Ohio River. Interestingly, this leaden plate has never been recovered. Although claimed by France, this region had been inhabited by Native Americans since prehistoric time.

Wheeling is the Delaware Indian word meaning "Place of the Head." It is believed that an early settler was killed by the Indians near the mouth of Wheeling Creek. His head was placed near the river as a graphic warning to other settlers that they were not welcome.

Ebenezer Zane officially founded Wheeling in 1769. Blessed with many natural resources, not least of which is the Ohio River, Wheeling became an important gateway to the West. It was the river which allowed Wheeling to grow as a center of transportation and industry in the first half of the nineteenth century. Elements of this early preeminence remain and can be found today throughout our city.

Among the various industries that were common in Wheeling's heyday were coal mining, iron and steel (the manufacture of cut nails led to the title of "Nail Capital of the World"), bricks, china and glass, tobacco (the famous Mail Pouch brand), and breweries.

This active industrial life attracted a large working class population. These workers, primarily European immigrants, were both craftsmen and laborers. The influences of these immigrants is still apparent in the architecture throughout the area and also in the recipes that have been handed down through families.

The Junior League of Wheeling, Inc. is proud to offer this collection of recipes, both old and new, as well as a glimpse of our rich heritage.

Appetizers
& Beverages

W H E E L I N G

Sweeney Punch Bowl

A monument in Greenwood Cemetery, Wheeling, once contained one of the largest pieces of cut lead crystal ever made. It is called the Sweeney Punch Bowl and was made in 1844 by brothers Michael and Thomas Sweeney. The nationally acclaimed bowl was placed in Michael's monument following his death in 1875. In 1949, the four-foot, ten-inch high, 225-pound Sweeney Punch Bowl was removed from the monument and placed on display at the Oglebay Institute Mansion Museum. It was moved again in 1993 to the new Oglebay Institute Glass Museum where it is housed in a facsimile of the original cemetery monument.

There was at least one, and perhaps two, other similar pieces of glass. A smaller bowl, made for Henry Clay, was ultimately destroyed in a fire. If there was a third piece, its history and whereabouts are unknown.

Chicken Cheese Ball

8 ounces cream cheese,
    softened
1 (4-ounce) can chunky
    chicken
1 teaspoon Worcestershire
    sauce
Onion powder to taste
1/2 cup crushed walnuts

Yield: 8 servings

- Combine cream cheese, chicken,
  Worcestershire sauce and onion powder in
  bowl; mix well.
- Shape into a ball. Roll in walnuts or pecans.
  Serve with crackers.

Cheryl Wilson

Olive Cheese Ball

8 ounces cream cheese,
    softened
8 ounces bleu cheese,
    crumbled
1/4 cup butter, softened
2/3 cup chopped black
    olives
1 tablespoon minced
    chives
1/3 cup toasted chopped
    almonds

Yield: 12 servings

- Combine cream cheese, bleu cheese and
  butter in bowl; mix well. Add olives and
  chives; mix well.
- Chill in refrigerator. Shape into a ball; place
  on serving dish. Chill until serving time.
- Sprinkle with almonds or chopped walnuts.
  Garnish with parsley; serve with crackers.

Sarah S. Miller

Apple Dip

16 ounces cream cheese,
    softened
1 cup packed brown sugar
1 cup caramel ice cream
    topping
1/2 cup coarsely chopped
    walnuts
1 pound Granny Smith
    apples, sliced
1 pound red Delicious
    apples, sliced

Yield: 12 servings

- Blend cream cheese and brown sugar in
  bowl. Spread on 12-inch pizza pan. Chill for
  30 minutes.
- Spread caramel topping over cream cheese
  layer; sprinkle with walnuts.
- Arrange apples in decorative pattern over
  top, alternating red and green slices.

Colleen Megna and Sherri K. Kellas

11

Mexican Bean Dip

1 (15-ounce) can refried
  beans
1/2 cup chopped onion
1 cup sour cream
1/2 envelope taco
  seasoning mix
1 (4-ounce) can sliced
  black olives
1 cup shredded Monterey
  Jack cheese

Yield: 12 servings

- Spread beans in 1-quart baking dish;
  sprinkle with onion.
- Combine sour cream and taco seasoning
  mix in small bowl; mix well. Spread over
  bean layer. Sprinkle with olives and cheese.
- Bake at 350 degrees for 15 minutes or until
  cheese melts. Serve with tortilla chips.

Nini Zadrozny

Cheesy Bacon and Green Pepper Dip

2 1/2 teaspoons Dijon
  mustard
3/4 cup mayonnaise
3/4 cup plain yogurt
2 cups finely shredded
  sharp Cheddar cheese
1 large green bell pepper,
  minced
1/2 cup thinly sliced green
  onions
5 slices bacon, crisp-fried,
  crumbled

Yield: 12 servings

- Combine mustard, mayonnaise, yogurt,
  cheese, green pepper, green onions and
  bacon in bowl; mix well.
- Chill until serving time. Serve with pita
  rounds or crackers.

Sarah H. Koeniger

Beth's Hot Beef Dip

4 ounces dried beef
1 pound Velveeta cheese,
  chopped
1 medium onion, chopped
2 tablespoons tomato
  sauce
1 tablespoon
  Worcestershire sauce
1/2 cup margarine
3 dashes of Tabasco sauce

Yield: 20 servings

- Rinse dried beef and pat dry; chop into
  small pieces.
- Combine beef with cheese, onion, tomato
  sauce, Worcestershire sauce, margarine and
  Tabasco sauce in double boiler. Cook over
  hot water until cheese and butter melt,
  stirring to mix well.
- Spoon into chafing dish. Serve with chips or
  vegetables for dipping.

Pat Kramer

More-Than-Curry Dip

1 cup mayonnaise
2 tablespoons Durkee
  Famous Sauce
1 tablespoon (heaping)
  horseradish
1 clove of garlic, minced
1/2 teaspoon
  Worcestershire sauce
Red pepper sauce to taste
1 teaspoon celery seeds
11/2 teaspoons curry
  powder
1 teaspoon seasoned salt

Yield: 8 servings

- Combine mayonnaise, Durkee sauce, horseradish, garlic, Worcestershire sauce, pepper sauce, celery seeds, curry powder and seasoned salt in bowl; mix well.
- Chill until serving time; flavor improves with time. Serve with crudités.
- May substitute Dijon mustard for Durkee sauce.

Jo Ellen Miller

Piña Colada Fruit Dip

8 ounces cream cheese,
  softened
2 envelopes piña colada
  mix
3 tablespoons rum
11/2 tablespoons milk
3 tablespoons sugar

Yield: 8 servings

- Combine cream cheese, piña colada mix, rum, milk and sugar in bowl; mix well.
- Chill until serving time. Serve with fresh fruit for dipping.

Beth Ann Dague

Potato Chip Dip

16 ounces cream cheese,
  softened
1 (2-ounce) jar chopped
  pimento
1/2 cup chopped onion
1/4 to 1/2 cup sugar
3/4 cup mayonnaise-type
  salad dressing
1/2 cup sour cream

Yield: 16 servings

- Combine cream cheese, undrained pimento, onion, sugar, mayonnaise and sour cream in bowl; mix well.
- Chill until serving time. Serve with potato chips or vegetables.
- May substitute 5 packets artificial sweetener for sugar.

Dorinda Lucas

Garden Salsa

This recipe was created to use the surplus of peppers and tomatoes from my father's garden.

8 cups chopped seeded
   peeled tomatoes
2 cups chopped green bell
   peppers
2 cups chopped hot
   banana peppers
1 cup chopped red pepper
2 cups chopped onions
3 tablespoons vinegar
3 tablespoons tarragon
   vinegar
2 teaspoons each
   tarragon, oregano and
   pepper

Yield: 12 pints

- Combine tomatoes, green peppers, banana peppers, red pepper, onions, vinegars, tarragon, oregano and pepper in stockpot.
- Bring to a boil; reduce heat. Simmer for 35 to 50 minutes or until of desired consistency. Cool to room temperature.
- Spoon into sterilized 1-pint jars, leaving ½ inch headspace; seal with 2-piece lids.
- May add 2 tablespoons chopped jalapeño peppers and ½ to 1 teaspoon crushed red chili pepper if desired.

Samantha Hensel Buch

Fresh Tomato Salsa

5 medium tomatoes,
   chopped
⅓ cup tomato sauce
¼ cup finely chopped
   purple onion
3 cloves of garlic, minced
1 or 2 small jalapeño
   peppers, seeded, minced
2 tablespoons chopped
   parsley
2 tablespoons lime juice
1 teaspoon oregano
1 teaspoon salt

Yield: 16 servings

- Combine tomatoes, tomato sauce, onion, garlic, peppers, parsley, lime juice, oregano and salt in bowl; mix gently.
- Chill, covered, until serving time. Serve with tortilla chips.

Stephanie W. Grove

Adena Indian burial mounds, shaped like Hershey kisses, dotted the banks of the Ohio River, Wheeling Creek, and such places as Wheeling Park. The Adena had inhabited this region since prehistoric time. Workmen on Water Street discovered a skeleton in 1848 believed to be an Indian chief. It was found in a sitting position and there was also an earthen jar, very neatly ornamented, nearby.

Shrimp Dip

1 (7-ounce) can tiny
  shrimp
1/2 cup mayonnaise
3 ounces cream cheese,
  softened
1/4 cup finely chopped
  celery
1/4 cup finely chopped
  green onions
1 1/2 tablespoons lemon
  juice
Red pepper to taste

Yield: 12 servings

- Rinse shrimp with warm water and drain.
- Blend mayonnaise and cream cheese in bowl. Add shrimp, celery, green onions, lemon juice and red pepper; mix well.
- Chill for several hours. Serve with Triscuits.

Pattie Hershey

Shrimp Dip Delight

16 ounces cream cheese,
  softened
1 (10-ounce) can cream of
  shrimp soup
1 small onion, finely
  chopped
1 (7-ounce) can tiny
  shrimp, drained

Yield: 15 servings

- Combine cream cheese, soup and onion in bowl; mix well. Fold in shrimp. Spoon into shallow baking dish.
- Bake, uncovered, at 350 degrees for 20 to 25 minutes or until heated through. Serve with crackers.

Dorothy Harman

Shrimp and Caper Spread

Keep the ingredients for this on hand to serve to unexpected guests.

1 (7-ounce) can tiny
  shrimp
1 (2-ounce) jar capers,
  drained
1/2 cup mayonnaise

Yield: 6 servings

- Rinse shrimp and drain. Combine with capers and mayonnaise in bowl; mix well.
- Serve with Melba toast or crackers.

Rosemary E. Miller

Egg and Caviar Sensation

12 hard-boiled eggs
1 medium onion
1/2 cup margarine,
  softened
1/2 cup mayonnaise
1/2 cup sour cream
1 (2-ounce) jar
  inexpensive caviar

Yield: 12 servings

- Grate eggs and onion into bowl. Add margarine and mayonnaise; mix well.
- Spoon into bowl lined with plastic wrap. Chill until serving time.
- Invert onto serving plate; remove plastic wrap. Spread with sour cream; sprinkle with caviar. Serve with Melba toast or crackers.

Pat Kramer

Texas Caviar

3/4 cup cider vinegar
1 tablespoon water
1/2 cup vegetable oil
1 cup sugar
1 teaspoon salt
1/2 teaspoon pepper
1 (15-ounce) can pinto
  beans
1 (15-ounce) can garbanzo
  beans
1 (15-ounce) can black
  beans
1 (15-ounce) can
  black-eyed peas
2 (11-ounce) cans white
  Shoe Peg corn
2 (4-ounce) cans chopped
  green chilies
1 (2-ounce) jar finely
  chopped pimento
1 cup finely chopped
  green bell pepper
1 cup finely chopped
  celery
1 small onion, finely
  chopped

Yield: 40 servings

- Combine vinegar, water, oil, sugar, salt and pepper in saucepan. Bring to a boil, stirring occasionally. Cool to room temperature.
- Drain beans, peas, corn, green chilies and pimento. Combine with green pepper, celery and onion in bowl. Add marinade; mix well.
- Chill, covered, for 24 hours. Serve with tortilla chips.

Paula Mertz

Layered Brie and Pesto

This is a beautiful presentation.

1 1/2 cups packed chopped
  fresh basil
1/2 cup packed chopped
  fresh parsley
3/4 cup grated Parmesan
  cheese or Romano
  cheese
1/4 cup pine nuts
2 cloves of garlic, cut into
  quarters
1/3 cup olive oil
8 ounces cream cheese,
  softened
4 to 5 ounces Brie cheese,
  rind removed
1/2 cup whipping cream,
  whipped

Yield: 16 servings

- Combine basil, parsley, Parmesan cheese, pine nuts and garlic in blender or food processor; process until coarsely chopped, scraping down sides. Add olive oil gradually, processing constantly until smooth. Chill in refrigerator.
- Blend cream cheese and Brie in mixer bowl. Fold in whipped cream.
- Line 4-cup mold with plastic wrap. Spread 1/4 of the cheese mixture in prepared mold. Layer pesto mixture and remaining cheese mixture 1/3 at a time in mold.
- Chill until serving time. Invert onto serving plate; remove plastic wrap. Serve with Melba toast or crackers.
- May add a layer of sun-dried tomatoes if desired.

Wendy F. Hinerman

Cranberry and Ginger Chutney

1 1/2 cups fresh cranberries
16 dried apricots, cut into
  quarters
1/3 cup chopped dates
2 tablespoons minced
  peeled ginger
3/4 cup packed light
  brown sugar
2 tablespoons orange juice
3/4 teaspoon cinnamon
1/4 teaspoon cayenne
  pepper

Yield: 12 servings

- Combine cranberries, apricots, dates, ginger, brown sugar, orange juice, cinnamon and cayenne pepper in heavy saucepan. Cook over medium heat until sugar dissolves, stirring constantly.
- Increase heat to high. Boil for 3 minutes. Spoon into bowl. Cool to room temperature.
- Store in airtight container in refrigerator for up to 1 week. Serve over Brie cheese. May also serve with chicken and pork.

Lou Crawford

Chutney Chicken Spread

1 envelope unflavored
  gelatin
1/2 cup milk
1 chicken bouillon cube
2 teaspoons curry powder
1 cup cream-style cottage
  cheese
3 ounces cream cheese,
  softened, cubed
1/2 cup sour cream
1 1/2 cups coarsely
  chopped cooked
  chicken breasts
1 (12-ounce) jar chutney
1/4 cup chopped celery
1 (2-ounce) jar chopped
  pimento, drained
1/3 cup chopped green
  onions
8 to 12 drops of Tabasco
  sauce
1/2 cup whipping cream

Yield: 12 servings

- Sprinkle gelatin over milk in small
  saucepan. Let stand for 5 minutes to soften.
  Add bouillon. Bring to a boil, stirring to
  dissolve gelatin and bouillon. Stir in curry
  powder. Cool slightly.
- Combine cottage cheese, cream cheese and
  sour cream in food processor fitted with
  metal blade; process until smooth. Add
  chicken, 1/2 cup of the chutney, celery,
  pimento, green onions, Tabasco sauce and
  gelatin mixture; process until coarsely
  chopped. Adjust seasonings.
- Whip cream in mixer bowl until soft peaks
  form. Fold in chicken mixture. Spoon into
  9-inch tart pan lined with plastic wrap.
  Chill until set.
- Place tart pan on serving plate; remove side
  of pan. Process remaining chutney in food
  processor until nearly smooth. Spread over
  congealed layer. Serve with crackers.
- May prepare in 9-inch quiche pan if
  preferred.

Donna Glass

Artichoke Pizazz

1 (14-ounce) can
  artichoke hearts,
  drained, chopped
1 cup grated Parmesan
  cheese
1 cup shredded
  mozzarella cheese
1 cup mayonnaise
2 tablespoons chopped
  green onions
1/2 teaspoon garlic powder

Yield: 6 servings

- Combine artichokes, cheeses, mayonnaise,
  green onions and garlic powder in bowl;
  mix well. Spoon into 1 1/2-quart baking dish.
- Bake, covered, at 350 degrees for 25 to 30
  minutes or until bubbly.

Anne D. Harman

Artichoke Phyllo Squares

2 (16-ounce) cans
   artichokes, drained,
   chopped
1 (15-ounce) container
   ricotta cheese
1 cup grated Parmesan
   cheese
1/4 cup chopped onion
2 tablespoons chopped
   parsley
1 egg
Tabasco sauce to taste
1/2 teaspoon salt
1/4 teaspoon pepper
1 (16-ounce) package
   frozen phyllo dough,
   thawed
1 1/4 cups melted margarine

Yield: 48 servings

- Combine artichokes, ricotta cheese,
Parmesan cheese, onion, parsley, egg,
Tabasco sauce, salt and pepper in bowl;
mix well.
- Place 1 sheet phyllo dough on buttered
9x13-inch baking dish; brush with
margarine. Fold in edges of phyllo to fit
dish. Repeat process until half the phyllo
dough is layered in dish.
- Spread artichoke filling in prepared dish.
Top with remaining phyllo dough, brushing
each layer with margarine.
- Cut into 48 squares with sharp knife. Bake
at 400 degrees for 20 to 30 minutes or until
golden brown.

Diana J. Davis

Bacon Wrap-Ups

10 slices dense white
   bread
8 ounces cream cheese,
   softened
1 tablespoon minced onion
10 slices bacon, cut into
   thirds

Yield: 30 servings

- Trim crusts from bread. Combine cream
cheese and onion in bowl; mix well. Spread
on bread; cut into thirds.
- Roll up each bread strip. Wrap each with 1
piece of bacon; secure with wooden pick.
Place on baking sheet.
- Bake at 350 degrees for 30 minutes or until
bacon is crisp, turning once.
- May add 1 tablespoon horseradish or
substitute horseradish for onion.

Gretchen Courtney Hooper

*Lewis Wetzel was considered the most famous scout of
the western border. He had the remarkable skill of being able to
load his musket while at a full run.*

Water Chestnut Appetizers

2 (5-ounce) cans water
chestnuts, drained
1 cup soy sauce
1/2 cup packed brown
sugar
1 pound thinly sliced
bacon, cut into thirds

Yield: 60 servings

- Cut water chestnuts into halves. Combine with soy sauce in bowl. Marinate in refrigerator for 30 minutes.
- Roll each water chestnut in brown sugar; wrap each with 1 piece bacon. Secure with wooden pick. Place on baking sheet.
- Bake at 350 degrees for 15 to 20 minutes or until bacon is nearly crisp. Broil for 3 to 4 minutes or until bacon is crisp; drain.

Syfra Bruhn

Cayenne Toasts

This is an excellent way to use leftover French bread.

1 cup olive oil
1 1/2 teaspoons sugar
1 teaspoon paprika
1 1/2 teaspoons each garlic
powder and onion
powder
1 1/2 teaspoons salt
2 teaspoons cayenne
pepper
1/2 teaspoon black pepper
3 loaves French bread

Yield: 18 servings

- Combine olive oil, sugar, paprika, garlic powder, onion powder, salt, cayenne pepper and black pepper in small bowl; whisk until smooth. Set aside.
- Slice French bread 1/4 inch thick; arrange in single layer on baking sheet. Brush with olive oil mixture, whisking oil constantly while using to mix seasonings.
- Toast at 200 degrees for 1 hour or until very crisp. Remove to wire rack to cool. Store in airtight container for up to 2 days. Serve with soups and salads.
- May freeze and reheat at 350 degrees for 5 to 7 minutes.

Christin Stein Bakewell

Friends of Wheeling, Inc. has worked to encourage historic preservation of the area's architecture. Friends of Wheeling worked with the Junior League on a painting and landscaping project in Centre Market.

Warm Cheese Bread

This is a crowd pleaser!

1 cup mayonnaise
1 cup grated Parmesan
  cheese
1 teaspoon minced garlic
1 round (1-pound) loaf
  sourdough bread
1/4 cup butter, softened
2 tablespoons finely
  chopped fresh basil

Yield: 8 to 10 servings

- Combine mayonnaise, cheese and garlic in bowl; mix well.
- Cut bread into halves horizontally. Place cut sides up on foil-lined baking sheet; spread with butter. Broil until crisp and brown.
- Spread mayonnaise mixture over bread. Broil until puffed and golden brown. Sprinkle with basil. Cut into wedges to serve.

Ange Lavy Joel

Roadhouse Wings

45 chicken wings
1/2 cup margarine
1 cup (or more) hot
  pepper sauce
Bleu Cheese Dressing
Celery sticks

Yield: 45 servings

- Cut each chicken wing into 3 portions, discarding tip portions. Rinse wings and pat dry; arrange in shallow baking pan.
- Bake at 375 degrees for 30 minutes or until brown and crisp; drain.
- Melt margarine in small saucepan. Stir in pepper sauce. Bring to a boil. Pour over wings, stirring to coat well.
- Serve warm with Bleu Cheese Dressing and celery sticks.

Judi Tarowsky

Bleu Cheese Dressing

4 ounces bleu cheese
2/3 cup mayonnaise
2/3 cup sour cream
1 tablespoon vinegar
1 tablespoon lemon juice
1/4 cup catsup
1/4 teaspoon salt

Yield: 45 servings

- Crumble bleu cheese into bowl. Add mayonnaise, sour cream, vinegar, lemon juice, catsup and salt; mix well.
- Chill for several hours before serving.

Carol Tyler

Parmesan Chicken

4 chicken breast filets
1 clove of garlic, minced
1/2 cup butter
1 tablespoon chopped
  parsley
1 teaspoon lemon juice
2 teaspoons Dijon mustard
1/8 teaspoon salt
1/4 cup bread crumbs
1/4 cup grated Parmesan
  cheese

Yield: 6 servings

• Cut chicken into 1 to 2-inch pieces; rinse and pat dry. Sauté with garlic in butter in skillet until no longer pink.
• Add parsley, lemon juice, mustard and salt; mix well. Remove from heat.
• Mix bread crumbs and cheese in bowl. Add to chicken, tossing to coat well.
• Spoon into baking dish. Bake, covered, at 325 to 350 degrees until cooked through and golden brown. Serve with wooden picks.

Kathy Parsons

Chilies Rellenos

3 or 4 (7-ounce) cans
  whole green chilies
1 pound Monterey Jack
  cheese, cut into strips
1 cup milk
2 eggs, slightly beaten
1 cup flour
1 teaspoon baking powder
3/4 cup cornmeal
1/2 teaspoon salt
Oil for deep frying

Yield: 8 servings

• Make a small slit in each chili pepper; remove and discard seeds. Place cheese in chilies.
• Blend milk and eggs in bowl. Add flour, baking powder, cornmeal and salt in bowl; mix well. Dip chilies into batter with large spoon.
• Deep-fry chilies in hot oil for 1 minute or just until golden brown; drain. Serve with red or green chili sauce; garnish with lettuce and tomato wedges.

Rosemary E. Miller

During a 1782 siege on Fort Henry, gunpowder supplies ran dangerously low. Betty Zane sprinted from the fort to Ebenezer Zane's cabin for more gunpowder, which was poured into her apron; thus ladened, she ran back to the fort.

Crab Meat Muffins

1 (5-ounce) jar Old
  English cheese
6 tablespoons margarine
2 tablespoons mayonnaise
1 (6-ounce) can crab
  meat, drained
1/2 teaspoon garlic powder
6 English muffins

Yield: 24 servings

- Combine cheese, margarine and mayonnaise in mixer bowl; beat until smooth. Add crab meat and garlic powder; mix well.
- Split muffins into halves. Spread cut sides with crab mixture. Cut each muffin into quarters; arrange on baking sheet.
- Broil for 5 minutes or until golden brown.
- May prepare muffins and freeze until time to broil.

Beth Brinker

Cocktail Meatballs

1 1/2 cups bread crumbs
1 cup milk
1 1/2 pounds ground chuck
1/2 cup chopped onion
1/4 cup chopped parsley
1 egg
1/2 teaspoon ginger
Salt to taste
1 (6-ounce) bottle of chili
  sauce
1 (6-ounce) jar grape jelly
3 tablespoons lemon juice

Yield: 12 servings

- Soak bread crumbs in milk in bowl. Add ground chuck, onion, parsley, egg, ginger and salt; mix well. Shape by tablespoonfuls into balls.
- Combine chili sauce, jelly and lemon juice in saucepan. Bring to a boil.
- Add meatballs. Simmer until meatballs are cooked through. Serve hot from chafing dish.

Roslyn Lando

Christmas was celebrated at the fort in 1783 with two large roasted turkeys and Twelfth-Day cake which was made of unleavened dough, slightly sweetened with spices, cloves and cinnamon bark worked into it, and then baked in a Dutch oven like a loaf of light bread. It was prepared a day or two in advance and eaten cold.

Mediterranean Treat

1 (12-ounce) jar roasted
  peppers, sliced
8 ounces feta cheese,
  crumbled
8 ounces fresh
  mushrooms, sliced
1 (8-ounce) jar oil-pack
  sun-dried tomatoes,
  drained, sliced
1 (16-ounce) can hearts of
  palm, drained, sliced
1 (16-ounce) package
  frozen phyllo dough,
  thawed
1/4 cup (about) olive oil

Yield: 11 servings

- Combine peppers, cheese, mushrooms, tomatoes and hearts of palm in bowl; mix well.
- Spread 1 sheet of phyllo dough on work surface; brush with olive oil. Fold dough into thirds. Spoon some of the filling onto end of dough. Fold dough to enclose filling, using triangular or flag fold. Place a second sheet of dough on work surface; brush with olive oil. Fold dough into thirds, sealing edges with olive oil. Place filled triangle on oiled dough; fold with flag fold. Repeat with remaining filling and dough.
- Prepare 11 triangles of foil, pinching up edges to form open triangular cups. Place 1 filled packet into each cup. Place on baking sheet. Freeze until firm.
- Bake frozen packets in foil cups at 350 degrees for 20 to 45 minutes or until golden brown.

Janie Altmeyer

Cajun Mushrooms

These are on the spicy side!

1 1/2 pounds small button
  mushrooms
1 cup unsalted butter
1 (5-ounce) bottle of
  Worcestershire sauce
5 to 6 drops of Tabasco
  sauce
1/2 teaspoon salt
1/4 cup finely ground
  pepper

Yield: 8 servings

- Sauté mushrooms in butter in heavy saucepan over medium heat. Stir in Worcestershire sauce, Tabasco sauce, salt and pepper. Increase heat to high.
- Cook, covered, for 20 minutes or until mushrooms are thickly glazed, stirring frequently. Remove to serving bowl with slotted spoon.

Christin Stein Bakewell

Mushroom Puffs

The easy flaky crust makes people think you have worked for hours.

1 pound mushrooms
1 tablespoon chopped
   onion
2 tablespoons butter
8 ounces cream cheese,
   softened
1 teaspoon garlic powder
1 teaspoon salt
1 (16-ounce) package
   frozen puff pastry
1 egg white, beaten

Yield: 24 servings

- Process mushrooms and onion in food processor until finely chopped. Sauté in butter in skillet until liquid has evaporated. Stir in cream cheese, garlic powder and salt.
- Prepare puff pastry using package directions. Arrange on lightly greased 10x15-inch baking sheet. Brush seams with egg white and seal. Spread with mushroom mixture.
- Bake at 350 degrees for 20 minutes. Cut into squares; serve warm.

Linda Elliott

Stuffed Mushrooms

1 pound mild sausage
2 tablespoons minced
   green bell pepper
1/4 cup minced onion
3 ounces cream cheese,
   softened
1/4 teaspoon
   Worcestershire sauce
1/2 teaspoon salt
1 pound fresh mushroom
   caps
1/2 cup soft bread crumbs
1 tablespoon butter
1 teaspoon chopped
   parsley

Yield: 40 servings

- Brown sausage in skillet, stirring until crumbly; drain and set aside.
- Combine green pepper and onion in 4-cup glass measure. Microwave, covered with paper towel, on High for 4 minutes, stirring once.
- Add sausage, cream cheese, Worcestershire sauce and salt; mix well.
- Spoon into mushroom caps; arrange stuffing side up on two 9-inch glass plates.
- Combine bread crumbs, butter and parsley in 2-cup glass measure. Microwave on High for 1 minute. Press mixture over tops of mushrooms.
- Microwave mushrooms 1/2 at a time on High for 1 to 2 minutes or until heated through.

Joan Grubler

Nachos Supreme

1 pound ground beef
1 envelope taco seasoning
  mix
1/4 cup hot water
1 (12-ounce) package
  tortilla chips
1 (12-ounce) can refried
  beans
3/4 cup medium salsa
1/2 cup sliced green onions
1/2 cup sliced black olives
1/2 cup nacho cheese sauce
1/4 cup sliced jalapeño
  peppers

Yield: 12 servings

- Brown ground beef in skillet, stirring until crumbly; drain. Add mixture of taco seasoning mix and water; mix well.
- Layer tortilla chips, ground beef mixture, refried beans, salsa, green onions, black olives, cheese sauce and peppers in 9x13-inch baking dish.
- Bake at 350 degrees for 20 minutes. Serve from baking dish with large spoon.

Colleen Megna

Smoked Oyster Roll

1 medium clove of garlic,
  crushed
1 medium shallot,
  chopped
16 ounces cream cheese,
  softened
2 tablespoons mayonnaise
2 teaspoons
  Worcestershire sauce
1/4 teaspoon Tabasco sauce
1/4 teaspoon salt
1/4 teaspoon white pepper
2 (4-ounce) cans smoked
  oysters, drained
1/2 cup finely chopped
  pecans

Yield: 8 servings

- Combine garlic, shallot, cream cheese, mayonnaise, Worcestershire sauce, Tabasco sauce, salt and pepper in food processor fitted with metal blade; process until smooth.
- Spread into 8x10-inch rectangle on foil.
- Process oysters in food processor until smooth. Spread over cream cheese layer. Chill, loosely covered with plastic wrap, for several hours or until firm.
- Loosen cream cheese layer from foil with long narrow spatula; roll as for jelly roll to enclose filling, smoothing cracks as necessary. Coat with pecans.
- Garnish roll with pimento strips and sprigs of parsley; serve with crackers. May chill, wrapped in plastic wrap, for up to 3 days.
- May substitute pistachios or walnuts for pecans.

Donna Glass

Party Ryes

8 ounces Cheddar cheese, shredded
1 (16-ounce) can pitted black olives, chopped
1 (3-ounce) jar bacon bits
1/2 cup mayonnaise
1 (4-ounce) can chopped green chilies
1 (4-ounce) jar jalapeño peppers, sliced
1 loaf party rye bread

Yield: 40 servings

- Combine cheese, olives, bacon bits, mayonnaise, green chilies and jalapeño peppers in large bowl; mix well.
- Spread on rye bread slices; arrange on baking sheet.
- Bake at 350 degrees for 7 to 8 minutes. May bake for 10 to 15 minutes or bake bread on 1 side before spreading for crisp ryes.
- May omit peppers if preferred.

Mary Lee Moore Bizanovich

Quick and Easy Pepperoni Rolls

1 (8-ounce) stick pepperoni
2 (10-count) cans buttermilk biscuits
8 ounces mozzarella cheese, shredded

Yield: 20 servings

- Cut pepperoni into 2-inch strips. Flatten each biscuit with hand on work surface. Place 2 strips pepperoni on each biscuit; sprinkle with cheese.
- Roll biscuits to enclose filling; press ends to seal. Place on baking sheet.
- Bake at 425 degrees for 10 to 13 minutes or until golden brown. Serve with warm pizza sauce for dipping if desired.
- May add your favorite vegetable, such as strips of green pepper or broccoli flowerets.

Missy Cunningham-O'Rourke

Samuel McColloch is remembered for his alleged leap from Wheeling Hill. The famous Indian Scout led forty men from a nearby fort to help defend Fort Henry in Wheeling during the 1777 siege. All of his men gained a safe entry into the fort except for Major McColloch, who was cut off by the attacking Indians. He rode to the top of Wheeling Hill only to be blocked by more Indians. With no other recourse, he rode his horse over the hillside. Both Samuel McColloch and his horse survived the 150-foot descent and escaped certain death.

Marinated Shrimp

1½ cups vegetable oil
¾ cup white vinegar
Several drops of Tabasco
 sauce
2½ teaspoons celery seeds
4 bay leaves
1½ teaspoons salt
5 pounds shrimp, cooked,
 peeled
2 cups sliced Bermuda
 onions

Yield: 20 servings

- Combine oil, vinegar, Tabasco sauce, celery seeds, bay leaves and salt in large bowl. Add shrimp and onions.
- Marinate, covered, in refrigerator for 24 hours, stirring occasionally. Remove shrimp to serving dish with slotted spoon. Garnish with some of the onions and watercress.

Wendy F. Hinerman

Cold Vegetable Pizza

2 (8-ounce) cans crescent
 rolls
16 ounces cream cheese,
 softened
3 tablespoons mayonnaise
½ teaspoon basil
¼ teaspoon garlic powder
2 cups mixed chopped
 tomatoes, green and red
 bell peppers, broccoli,
 cucumbers and radishes
2 cups shredded Cheddar
 cheese

Yield: 30 servings

- Unroll dough and place on 10x15-inch baking sheet, pressing edges and perforations to seal. Bake at 350 degrees for 12 to 15 minutes or until golden brown.
- Combine cream cheese, mayonnaise, basil and garlic powder in bowl; mix until smooth. Spread over crust.
- Sprinkle with vegetables and cheese. Cut into squares to serve.
- May substitute vegetables of choice for topping.

Stephanie W. Grove

Ebenezer Zane sold building lots in 1792. If the owner did not build a house in seven years, the property was forfeited for use by the town.

Early Wheeling City councilmen were called the "Housekeepers."

Seasoned Oyster Crackers

2 (16-ounce) packages
  oyster crackers
1 cup vegetable oil
2 envelopes buttermilk
  ranch salad dressing mix
1 envelope original ranch
  salad dressing mix
1/4 teaspoon garlic powder
1 teaspoon dillweed
1/4 teaspoon lemon pepper

Yield: 25 servings

- Place crackers in 4-quart baking pan.
- Combine oil, salad dressing mixes, garlic powder, dillweed and lemon pepper in bowl; mix well. Drizzle over crackers, stirring to coat well.
- Bake at 250 degrees for 30 minutes, stirring after 15 minutes. Drain on paper towels. Cool completely. Store in airtight container.

Martha S. Beneke

Seasoned Pumpkin Seeds

3/4 cup pumpkin seeds
1 tablespoon light butter
1/2 tablespoon
  Worcestershire sauce
1/2 tablespoon seasoned
  salt

Yield: 4 servings

- Wash pumpkin seeds well and pat dry. Sprinkle in 9-inch baking dish. Add butter, Worcestershire sauce and seasoned salt; mix well.
- Microwave on High for 8 minutes or until seeds are dry and lightly toasted, stirring every 2 minutes; do not overcook.

Emily S. Fisher

Bloody Marys

These are a New Year's Day tradition.

2 cups vegetable juice
  cocktail
2 cups tomato juice
2 teaspoons
  Worcestershire sauce
2 teaspoons lemon juice
2 dashes bitters
Garlic salt to taste
2 cups vodka

Yield: 8 servings

- Combine vegetable juice cocktail, tomato juice, Worcestershire sauce, lemon juice, bitters, garlic salt and vodka in pitcher; mix gently.
- Serve over ice; garnish with celery stalks.

Robert C. Miller

The Morning Energizer

1/2 cup plain nonfat yogurt
3/4 cup orange juice
1/2 cup chopped apple
1/2 banana, chopped
2 tablespoons peanut
  butter
1/4 cup wheat germ
Grated lemon rind to taste
1/2 teaspoon cinnamon
1 teaspoon vanilla extract

Yield: 4 servings

• Combine yogurt, orange juice, apple, banana, peanut butter, wheat germ, lemon rind, cinnamon and vanilla in blender container.
• Add ice. Process until smooth. Pour into glasses.

Hali Exley

The Replenisher

Sections of 2 oranges
2 bananas
1 tablespoon honey
1/2 cup nonfat milk
1 tablespoon lemon juice
1 teaspoon vanilla extract

Yield: 2 servings

• Combine oranges, bananas, honey, milk, lemon juice and vanilla in blender container.
• Add ice. Process until smooth. Pour into glasses.

Hali Exley

Cranberry Snap Punch

1 quart cranberry juice
2 cups fresh orange juice
1/2 cup fresh lemon juice
1 cup pineapple juice
1/2 cup drained crushed
  pineapple
1 cup water
1/3 cup sugar
1 teaspoon almond extract

Yield: 12 servings

• Combine cranberry juice, orange juice, lemon juice, pineapple juice, pineapple, water, sugar and almond extract in large container.
• Chill until serving time. Serve over crushed ice.

Beth Ann Dague

In the early 1800s, tea was made from goldenrod, coffee from parched corn or barley, and homemade molasses and sugar were made from the sap of maple trees.

Perfectly Pink Punch

1 quart raspberry sherbet
2 quarts ginger ale
1 quart cranberry juice
1 (32-ounce) can
  pineapple juice

Yield: 24 servings

- Soften sherbet in punch bowl. Add ginger ale, cranberry juice and pineapple juice; mix gently.
- Ladle into punch cups.

Bonnie Ritz

Freezer Daiquiris

3 (12-ounce) cans frozen
  lemonade concentrate,
  thawed
1 (12-ounce) can frozen
  limeade concentrate,
  thawed
7 cups water
1 fifth light rum

Yield: 16 servings

- Combine lemonade concentrate, limeade concentrate, water and rum in 1-gallon plastic container; mix well.
- Freeze for 48 hours. Mix well and scoop into glasses to serve.

Wendy F. Hinerman

Mock Champagne

Perfect for toasting the mom-to-be at a baby shower

4 cups apple juice
8 cups carbonated
  lemon-lime drink

Yield: 16 servings

- Combine apple juice and lemon-lime drink in punch bowl; mix gently.
- May make in any amounts needed, using 1 part apple juice to 2 parts lemon-lime drink.

Cookbook Committee

*During the period when Wheeling was a wide-open city,
a raid produced $106 for each prostitute arrested.*

Raspberry Champagne Punch

2 (10-ounce) packages
 frozen red raspberries
 in syrup, thawed
1/3 cup lemon juice
1/2 cup sugar
1 (750-milliliter) bottle of
 rosé, chilled
1 (750-milliliter) bottle of
 Champagne, chilled
1 quart raspberry sherbet,
 softened

Yield: 16 servings

- Purée raspberries in blender or food
 processor. Combine with lemon juice, sugar
 and rosé in punch bowl; stir to dissolve
 sugar.
- Add Champagne and sherbet just before
 serving; mix gently.

Beth Ann Dague

Raspberry Wine Punch

1 large bottle of raspberry
 wine
1 (2-liter) bottle of 7-Up
1 (2-liter) bottle of ginger
 ale

Yield: 40 servings

- Chill wine, 7-Up and ginger ale. Combine
 in punch bowl; mix gently.
- Add ice ring made of additional ginger ale
 and fresh fruit such as raspberries,
 pineapple, lemon and orange. Garnish with
 fresh mint.

Kathy B. Santilli

*In the summertime, before the locks and dams were constructed,
the Ohio River would drop to ankle depth. Wheelingites would wade in the
river to salvage coal that had dropped from the steamboats and use it
to heat their homes in the winter. An 1840 city ordinance prohibited bathing in
the Ohio River or Wheeling Creek from sunrise until one hour after sunset.*

Kahlua Coffee Hummers

This looks very pretty in brandy or red wine glasses.

1 quart coffee ice cream
1/4 cup brandy
1/4 cup Kahlua
Cinnamon to taste

Yield: 4 servings

- Combine ice cream, brandy and Kahlua in food processor; process to consistency of thick milk shake.
- Pour into glasses; sprinkle with cinnamon.

Mary W. Renner

Margaritas

6 tablespoons Tequila
3 tablespoons Triple Sec
2 tablespoons sweet and sour drink mix
1 (6-ounce) can frozen limeade concentrate, thawed
4 cups ice

Yield: 4 servings

- Combine Tequila, Triple Sec, drink mix, limeade concentrate and ice in blender container; process until smooth.
- Rub rims of glasses with lime and dip into salt. Pour Margaritas into glasses.

Beth Ann Dague

The 1816 Wheeling-built steamboat, the Washington, was the fourth steam vessel to travel down the Ohio River. The design of the Washington served as the prototype of the steamers which plied the western rivers. A curious attraction on the Ohio River was Hornbrook's steamboat which was outfitted with shelves and counters to serve as a general store. Most anything could be purchased there, from an ax handle to a Sunday-go-to-meeting dress.

White Sangria Slush

This is great for when the girls get together.

1 (12-ounce) can frozen
   lemonade concentrate,
   thawed
1 (6-ounce) can frozen
   orange juice
   concentrate, thawed
1 1/2 cups water
1 (750-milliliter) bottle of
   dry white wine
1 (10-ounce) bottle of
   club soda, chilled
Lemon, lime or orange
   slices

Yield: 12 servings

• Combine lemonade concentrate, orange
  juice concentrate and water in bowl; mix
  well. Pour into freezer pan. Freeze until
  slushy.
• Spoon slush into large pitcher. Add wine
  and club soda; mix gently. Garnish with
  lemon, lime or orange slices.

Roanne M. Burech

Hot Buttered Rum

1 (1-pound) package
   brown sugar
1 (1-pound) package
   confectioners' sugar
1 teaspoon each nutmeg
   and cinnamon
2 cups melted butter
1 quart vanilla ice cream,
   softened
Rum to taste

Yield: variable

• Stir brown sugar, confectioners' sugar,
  nutmeg and cinnamon into melted butter in
  bowl. Stir in ice cream. Store in refrigerator.
• Place 2 tablespoons of ice cream mixture in
  each mug. Add rum to taste and enough hot
  water to fill mug, stirring to mix well.

Ella Jane Howard

Hot Cranberry Punch

3/4 cup packed brown
   sugar
1 teaspoon whole cloves
4 (1 1/2-inch) cinnamon
   sticks
1 1/2 quarts cranberry juice
   cocktail
1 quart apple juice

Yield: 20 servings

• Place brown sugar, cloves and cinnamon
  sticks in filter basket of electric coffee
  percolator.
• Combine cranberry juice cocktail and apple
  juice in percolator. Run through percolator
  cycle. Serve hot.

Beth Ann Dague

Soups & Sandwiches

W H E E L I N G

West Virginia Independence Hall

Originally used as a federal Custom House, the building located at 16th and Market streets, opened in 1859. The style of the building is Italian Renaissance Revival, and the material chosen for the building was sandstone. The architect, Ammi B. Young, designed this building to be as fireproof as possible. Interestingly, the doors were made wide enough to accommodate the hoop skirts of the era.

On June 20, 1861, the Restored Government of Virginia was formed in the courtroom of the Custom House, Wheeling. This government chose to remain loyal to the Union, while the Commonwealth of Virginia, in Richmond, pledged its allegiance to the Confederacy. The Restored Government of Virginia used the Custom House as its capitol building. At this time, there were two capitals of Virginia: the original capital, Richmond, and Wheeling. Constitutional law required the government of Virginia to grant permission for a separate state to be formed from within its boundaries. The delegates in Washington were those from the Restored Government of Virginia. They voted as Virginia, and granted permission to form the new state of West Virginia. The state of West Virginia was officially born June 20, 1863.

After extensive restoration, West Virginia Independence Hall, formerly the Custom House, was designated a National Historic Landmark by the United States Department of the Interior.

photograph courtesy of the Oglebay Institute Mansion Museum

Tailgate Beer Cheese Soup

Great for tailgate football parties on cold autumn days

1/4 cup unsalted butter
1/2 cup finely chopped
  celery
1/2 cup finely chopped
  leeks
1/2 cup finely chopped
  carrots
1/4 cup flour
4 cups beef broth
1 (12-ounce) can beer
1 pound white Cheddar
  cheese, chopped
1 pound sharp Cheddar
  cheese, chopped
Cayenne pepper to taste
Salt and black pepper to
  taste
1/2 cup croutons
Minced fresh parsley or
  chives to taste
Bacon for garnish

Yield: 6 servings

- Melt butter in stockpot. Stir in celery, leeks and carrots. Cook over low heat for 3 minutes, stirring constantly.
- Stir in flour. Cook over low heat for 2 minutes, stirring constantly.
- Add broth and beer; mix well. Simmer for 15 to 20 minutes or until vegetables are tender, stirring occasionally.
- Add cheeses gradually. Simmer until smooth, stirring constantly. Season with cayenne pepper, salt and black pepper. Simmer until heated through; do not boil.
- Spoon into wide-mouthed thermos. Serve in mugs topped with croutons, parsley and bacon.

Ann Vieweg

Broccoli and Mushroom Soup

4 chicken bouillon cubes
4 cups hot water
1 pound fresh broccoli,
  cut into 1/2-inch pieces
1 cup margarine
1 cup sifted flour
2 cups milk
8 ounces fresh
  mushrooms, sliced
Pepper to taste

Yield: 8 servings

- Dissolve bouillon cubes in hot water; mix well.
- Steam broccoli in steamer until tender-crisp.
- Melt margarine in saucepan. Stir in flour. Cook for 2 to 4 minutes or until smooth, stirring constantly. Add bouillon; mix well.
- Bring to a boil; reduce heat. Stir in broccoli, milk, mushrooms and pepper.
- Cook just until heated through, stirring constantly. Ladle into soup bowls.

Melissa Lucas Graham

Butternut and Leek Bisque

Pretty and tasty!

2 pounds butternut
  squash, cut into halves
2 large leeks
1¹/₂ teaspoons olive oil
1 small apple, peeled,
  chopped
2 cups water
1 (14-ounce) can
  low-sodium chicken
  broth
1¹/₂ teaspoons salt
¹/₄ teaspoon sage
¹/₄ teaspoon white pepper
¹/₈ teaspoon allspice
³/₄ cup half and half or
  milk

Yield: 4 servings

- Prick squash with fork. Place cut side down in baking pan. Bake at 400 degrees for 45 minutes or until tender. Cool. Scrape pulp into bowl.
- Trim leeks, leaving 2 inches of green; chop.
- Sauté leeks in oil in saucepan over medium heat for 8 minutes. Stir in squash, apple, water, broth and seasonings.
- Simmer for 15 minutes or until vegetables are tender, stirring occasionally.
- Process in several batches in blender or food processor until smooth.
- Bring bisque to a simmer in saucepan just before serving. Stir in half and half. Simmer just until heated through, stirring frequently.
- Ladle into soup bowls.

Mary W. Renner

Chicken Soup with Rice and Sausage

8 ounces turkey sausage
  links
1 (3-pound) chicken, cut up
4 cups chicken broth
2 cloves of garlic, chopped
1 bay leaf
1¹/₂ teaspoons salt
1 teaspoon thyme
¹/₂ teaspoon pepper
2 large potatoes, chopped
2 (16-ounce) cans diced
  tomatoes
1 large onion, chopped
1 cup frozen whole kernel
  corn
¹/₄ teaspoon liquid red
  pepper seasoning
2 cups white rice, cooked

Yield: 8 servings

- Brown sausage in skillet over medium-high heat; drain. Cut into ¹/₂-inch slices.
- Rinse chicken. Combine with next 6 ingredients in stockpot; mix well. Bring to a boil; reduce heat. Simmer, covered, for 25 minutes or until chicken is tender.
- Remove chicken to platter.
- Skim fat from broth. Chop chicken, discarding skin and bones.
- Add potatoes to broth. Simmer until tender. Stir in tomatoes, onion and sausage, corn, red pepper seasoning, rice and chicken.
- Simmer, covered, for 10 minutes, stirring occasionally. Discard bay leaf.
- Ladle into soup bowls.

Mary W. Renner

Aunt Shirl's Cajun Chili

1 large onion, chopped
5 or 6 cloves of garlic,
  finely chopped
2 tablespoons vegetable oil
1½ to 2 pounds ground
  beef
Salt and pepper to taste
3 (16-ounce) cans chili
  beans
1 (28-ounce) can whole
  tomatoes, mashed
1 (28-ounce) can tomato
  purée
2 envelopes chili
  seasoning mix
3 to 6 ounces beer
2 tablespoons cumin
2 tablespoons chili powder
1 cup shredded Cheddar
  cheese

Yield: 6 servings

- Sauté onion and garlic in oil in stockpot. Stir in ground beef, salt and pepper. Cook until ground beef is crumbly, stirring constantly; drain.
- Add undrained chili beans, undrained tomatoes, tomato purée and seasoning mix; mix well.
- Bring to a boil; do not stir. Reduce heat. Simmer for 1 hour or until thickened, stirring occasionally.
- Stir in beer. Season with salt, pepper, cumin and chili powder.
- Simmer for 30 minutes, stirring occasionally.
- Ladle into soup bowls; sprinkle with cheese. Serve with tortilla chips.

Lori Dallas

Cincinnati Chili

2 pounds lean ground beef
4 cups water
2 (8-ounce) cans tomato
  sauce
1 tablespoon allspice
¼ cup chili powder
1 teaspoon cumin
½ ounce unsweetened
  chocolate
3 cloves of garlic, chopped
2 tablespoons vinegar
1 bay leaf
1½ teaspoons salt
2 tablespoons
  Worcestershire sauce
1 teaspoon cinnamon
2 whole cloves
1 (16-ounce) package
  spaghetti, cooked,
  drained

Yield: 8 servings

- Combine ground beef, water, tomato sauce, allspice, chili powder, cumin, chocolate, garlic, vinegar, bay leaf, salt, Worcestershire sauce, cinnamon and cloves in stockpot; mix well.
- Simmer for 3 hours, stirring occasionally.
- Chill, covered, overnight; skim off fat.
- Cook just until heated through, stirring occasionally. Discard bay leaf.
- Serve over hot cooked spaghetti. Garnish with chopped onion, kidney beans and shredded Cheddar cheese. Serve with oyster crackers.

Debbie Lucki

Slow-Cooker Chili

Put this in the slow cooker before you leave to spend a day antiquing.

2¹/₂ pounds ground beef
2 tablespoons dried
    minced onion
2 tablespoons chili powder
¹/₂ teaspoon freshly
    ground pepper
1 teaspoon salt
3 cloves of garlic, minced
1 (6-ounce) can tomato
    paste
1¹/₂ cups tomato juice
1 (16-ounce) can kidney
    beans, drained
1 (16-ounce) can
    tomatoes, chopped
1 cup chopped celery
1 cup chopped green bell
    pepper

Yield: 6 servings

- Brown ground beef in skillet, stirring until crumbly; drain.
- Combine ground beef, onion, chili powder, pepper, salt, garlic, tomato paste, tomato juice, kidney beans, undrained tomatoes, celery and green pepper in slow cooker; mix well.
- Cook on Low for 7 to 9 hours or until of desired consistency, stirring occasionally. May add additional liquid if needed.
- Ladle into soup bowls.

Gail E. Carl

Vegetarian Chili

2 (16-ounce) cans kidney
    beans, drained
1 (8-ounce) can tomato
    sauce
4 cloves of garlic, crushed
1¹/₂ cups chopped onions
2 tablespoons olive oil
1 cup each chopped celery,
    carrots and green bell
    pepper
1 (15-ounce) can chopped
    tomatoes
1 teaspoon lemon juice
1 teaspoon cumin
1 teaspoon basil
2 tablespoons chili powder
¹/₂ cup dry red wine
Red pepper sauce to taste
1 cup shredded Cheddar
    cheese

Yield: 8 servings

- Combine kidney beans and tomato sauce in slow cooker; mix well.
- Sauté garlic and onions in olive oil in skillet. Stir in celery, carrots and green pepper. Cook until vegetables are tender, stirring constantly.
- Stir garlic mixture into bean mixture. Add undrained tomatoes, lemon juice, cumin, basil, chili powder, red wine and red pepper sauce; mix well.
- Cook on Low for 1 hour or until of desired consistency.
- Ladle into soup bowls: sprinkle with cheese.

Cheryl Danehart

Clam Chowder

4 (6-ounce) cans chopped
  clams
4 ounces bacon, chopped
2 medium onions, chopped
3 ribs celery, chopped
2 green bell peppers,
  chopped
6 medium potatoes,
  chopped
2 bay leaves
1 teaspoon thyme
1 teaspoon celery salt
Pepper to taste
3 tablespoons butter
3 tablespoons flour
2 cups half and half

Yield: 8 servings

- Drain clams, reserving liquid.
- Fry bacon in stockpot until crisp, stirring
  frequently. Remove bacon to bowl.
- Sauté onions, celery and green peppers in
  pan drippings until brown. Stir in potatoes
  and clams. Add enough water to reserved
  clam liquid to measure 3 cups. Stir into
  clam mixture.
- Cook over medium heat until potatoes are
  tender, stirring occasionally. Stir in
  seasonings. Melt butter in saucepan. Stir in
  flour. Add half and half gradually; mix well.
  Stir into clam mixture.
- Cook for 10 minutes, stirring frequently.
  Chill in refrigerator. Cook just until heated
  through, stirring constantly. Remove bay
  leaves. Ladle into soup bowls; sprinkle with
  bacon.

Susie Pere

Elegant Pimento Soup

This subtle soup makes an elegant first course.

1 (16-ounce) jar
  pimentos, drained,
  chopped
2 cups chicken broth
5 tablespoons butter
1/4 cup flour
3 cups half and half
3 cups chicken broth
Salt and pepper to taste
1/2 cup sour cream

Yield: 8 servings

- Bring pimentos and 2 cups broth to a
  simmer in saucepan. Purée mixture in
  blender or food processor. Set aside.
- Melt butter in saucepan. Stir in flour. Cook
  until bubbly, stirring constantly. Add half
  and half gradually. Simmer for 3 minutes or
  until thickened, stirring constantly. Stir in
  puréed mixture and 3 cups broth.
- Simmer for 3 minutes or just until heated
  through. Season with salt and pepper.
- Ladle into soup bowls; top with sour cream.
  Garnish with watercress, dill, parsley or
  chives. May serve chilled.

Ann Vieweg

Italian Wedding Soup

2 whole chicken breasts
4 quarts water
3 cups chopped celery
1 medium onion, chopped
1/3 cup chopped fresh
   parsley
Pepper to taste
4 chicken bouillon cubes
1 small head escarole
1 pound lean ground beef
1/3 cup chopped fresh
   parsley
1 egg, beaten
1/3 cup grated Romano
   cheese
1/4 cup chopped onion
3/4 teaspoon salt
3/4 cup bread crumbs
1/2 cup pastina
1 egg, beaten
1/3 cup grated Romano
   cheese

Yield: 16 servings

- Rinse chicken. Combine chicken, water, celery, 1 onion, 1/3 cup parsley, pepper and bouillon cubes in stockpot; mix well.
- Cook until chicken is tender.
- Remove chicken to platter. Chop, discarding skin and bones. Return to stockpot.
- Bring escarole and enough water to cover to a boil in large saucepan. Boil for 7 minutes; drain. Chop escarole. Stir into chicken mixture.
- Combine ground beef, pepper, 1/3 cup parsley, 1 egg, 1/3 cup Romano cheese, 1/4 cup onion, salt and bread crumbs in bowl; mix well. Shape into 1/2-inch balls.
- Bring chicken mixture to a boil; add meatballs. Stir in pastina.
- Simmer for 20 minutes or until pastina is done, stirring occasionally.
- Bring soup to a boil just before serving. Stir in 1 egg and 1/3 cup Romano cheese. Ladle into soup bowls immediately.

Nini Zadrozny

Mushroom Velvet Soup

8 ounces mushrooms,
   sliced
1 medium onion, chopped
1/3 cup chopped fresh
   parsley
1/4 cup butter
1 tablespoon flour
1 (14-ounce) can beef
   broth
1 cup sour cream

Yield: 4 servings

- Sauté mushrooms, onion and parsley in butter in skillet for 5 minutes or until mushrooms are tender and liquids are absorbed.
- Stir in flour. Cook for 1 minute or until brown, stirring constantly. Add broth gradually; mix well.
- Bring mixture to a boil, stirring constantly.
- Pour into blender or food processor container. Add sour cream.
- Process until smooth. Pour into saucepan.
- Cook just until heated through, stirring constantly. Ladle into soup bowls.

Ruth B. Mann

Nonfat Red and White Soup

3 cups chopped red bell
pepper
2 cups chopped green bell
pepper
4 cups chopped potatoes
2 cups chopped purple
onions
4 cups water
2 (15-ounce) cans tomato
sauce
1 cup white wine
1 teaspoon cinnamon
1/2 teaspoon cayenne
pepper
1 teaspoon cumin
1/2 cup chopped fresh
cilantro

Yield: 14 servings

- Bring red pepper, green pepper, potatoes, purple onions and water to a boil in stockpot; reduce heat.
- Simmer, covered, for 30 minutes or until potatoes are tender, stirring occasionally.
- Stir in tomato sauce, white wine, cinnamon, cayenne pepper, cumin and cilantro.
- Bring to a boil; reduce heat. Simmer, covered, for 15 minutes.
- Process mixture 1/2 at a time in food processor until smooth.
- Ladle into soup bowls. Garnish with nonfat plain yogurt and cilantro sprigs.
- Serve with a salad topped with nonfat salad dressing and low-fat bread.

Holly A. Fluty

Potato Soup

1 onion, chopped
2 tablespoons butter
2 ribs celery, chopped
2 carrots, chopped
6 potatoes, chopped
3 cups water
5 chicken bouillon cubes
3/4 teaspoon seasoned salt
1/2 teaspoon thyme
1/2 teaspoon rosemary
Garlic powder to taste
Pepper to taste
2 cups skim milk
1 cup shredded longhorn
cheese

Yield: 6 servings

- Sauté onion in butter in stockpot. Stir in celery, carrots, potatoes, water, bouillon cubes, seasoned salt, thyme, rosemary, garlic powder and pepper; mix well.
- Simmer for 20 minutes, stirring occasionally; mash vegetables.
- Stir in skim milk and cheese. Cook until cheese melts, stirring constantly.
- Serve with a salad and bread.

Nancy Peluchette

Thomas U. Walter, architect of the U.S. Capitol, designed a bank for Wheeling.
In 1837, he charged the bank $125.00 for the plans and description.

Tomato Soup

This is fabulous!

1 peck tomatoes, cut into
  quarters
1 green bell pepper,
  chopped
1/2 to 1 hot pepper,
  chopped
3 large onions, chopped
3 ribs celery, chopped
1/2 cup butter
2/3 cup sugar
5 tablespoons cornstarch
2 tablespoons salt
1 cup tomato juice

Yield: 12 servings

- Cook tomatoes in stockpot until soft,
  stirring occasionally.
- Sauté green pepper, hot pepper, onions and
  celery in butter in skillet. Add to tomatoes;
  mix well.
- Process tomato mixture in small batches in
  blender or food processor until puréed.
  Press through sieve, discarding seeds.
- Return tomato mixture to stockpot. Stir in
  mixture of sugar, cornstarch, salt and
  tomato juice.
- Bring soup to a boil. Ladle into soup bowls.

Julie Squibb

Creamy Tomato Soup

Wonderful! And tomatoes do not have to be in season.

1 small onion, finely
  chopped
1 small carrot, finely
  chopped
2 tablespoons margarine
1 (28-ounce) can tomatoes
1/2 teaspoon basil
1/2 teaspoon thyme
Salt and pepper to taste
1 cup whipping cream
Chopped fresh parsley to
  taste

Yield: 4 servings

- Sauté onion and carrot in margarine in
  2-quart saucepan until onion is tender. Add
  tomatoes, basil, thyme, salt and pepper; mix
  well. Bring to a boil; reduce heat.
- Simmer, covered, for 20 minutes, stirring
  occasionally.
- Process tomato mixture in food processor or
  blender until puréed. Return puréed
  mixture to saucepan.
- Whisk in whipping cream. Cook just until
  heated through, stirring constantly.
- Ladle into soup bowls; sprinkle with parsley.
- May serve chilled. May double recipe.

Ruth B. Mann

Turkey and Barley Chowder

4 whole cloves
4 whole peppercorns
2 cups chopped cooked
  turkey
2 (14-ounce) cans chicken
  broth
1 (15-ounce) can tomato
  sauce with tomato bits
1/4 cup medium pearl
  barley
1 medium onion, thinly
  sliced
1 cup water
1 1/2 teaspoons sugar
1 tablespoon sherry
1/2 cup half and half

Yield: 6 servings

- Tie cloves and peppercorns in cheesecloth.
- Combine cloves mixture, turkey, broth, tomato sauce, barley, onion, water and sugar in large saucepan; mix well.
- Simmer, covered, for 1 hour or until barley is tender, stirring occasionally.
- Stir in sherry and half and half. Cook just until heated through, stirring constantly; do not boil. Discard cheesecloth bag.
- Ladle into soup bowls.
- May substitute chicken for turkey.

Hali Exley

Slow-Cooker Vegetable Soup

Good for a busy day!

1 pound beef stew meat
2 teaspoons salt
1 1/2 teaspoons
  Worcestershire sauce
Pepper to taste
2 teaspoons parsley flakes
1 small onion, chopped
1 (10-ounce) package
  frozen cut green beans
1 cup chopped celery
1 cup sliced carrots
1 cup chopped peeled
  potato
1 (16-ounce) can whole
  tomatoes
1 (10-ounce) package
  frozen whole kernel
  corn

Yield: 6 servings

- Combine stew meat, salt, Worcestershire sauce, pepper, parsley flakes, onion, green beans, celery, carrots, potato, undrained tomatoes and corn in slow cooker; mix well. Add just enough water to cover; mix well.
- Cook on High for 8 hours, stirring occasionally.
- Ladle into soup bowls

Gail E. Carl

Vegetable Soup

2 large onions, sliced
3 carrots, sliced
3 ribs celery, sliced
3 tablespoons vegetable oil
3 potatoes, chopped
2 cups fresh green beans
1/2 head cabbage, shredded
1 (28-ounce) can whole
   tomatoes, chopped
4 cups beef broth
4 cups chicken broth
1/2 teaspoon thyme
1/2 teaspoon marjoram
1 (8-ounce) can peas
1 1/2 cups cooked macaroni

Yield: 16 servings

- Sauté onions, carrots and celery in oil in stockpot for 10 minutes.
- Add potatoes, uncooked green beans, cabbage, undrained tomatoes, beef broth, chicken broth, thyme and marjoram; mix well.
- Simmer until vegetables are tender, stirring occasionally. Stir in peas and macaroni.
- Cook for 5 minutes, stirring occasionally.
- Ladle into soup bowls. Serve with slices of French bread which have been buttered, sprinkled with Parmesan cheese and toasted.

Kathy A. Blass

Cajun Chicken Sandwiches

1 1/2 pounds chicken
   breast filets
1 long loaf sourdough
   bread
1 small onion, chopped
1/2 teaspoon Cajun
   seasoning
Salt to taste
1 cup shredded
   mozzarella cheese

Yield: 4 servings

- Rinse chicken and pat dry; chop.
- Slice bread loaf lengthwise 3/4 of the way through; cut crosswise into 4 sections.
- Sauté chicken in nonstick skillet until light brown. Stir in onion and Cajun seasoning. Cook until onion is tender, stirring constantly. Season with salt.
- Stuff each bread segment with chicken mixture; sprinkle top with cheese. Place on baking sheet.
- Bake at 325 degrees for 5 minutes or until cheese melts.
- Serve with shredded lettuce, chopped tomato and horseradish sauce.

Cindy Richards

More than eighteen thousand people were fed during the 1840 Whig meeting for Harrison and Tyler. Wheeling Hill "from its eastern extremity for about a quarter of a mile to the northwest was one grand hotel table." Food included cold beef, ham, tongue, vegetables, bread, cheese, pies, barrels of ice water and much more.

Crab Sandwiches

These open-faced sandwiches make a good luncheon entrée.

8 slices tomato
Salt to taste
8 slices sharp Cheddar
   cheese
8 Holland rusks
1 pound crab meat,
   drained, flaked
8 ounces cream cheese,
   softened
2 tablespoons mayonnaise
1 tablespoon lemon juice
1/2 teaspoon
   Worcestershire sauce
1 tablespoon grated onion
Tabasco sauce to taste

Yield: 8 servings

- Sprinkle tomato slices with salt. Layer cheese slices and tomato slices in order listed on rusks.
- Combine crab meat, cream cheese, mayonnaise, lemon juice, Worcestershire sauce, onion and Tabasco sauce in bowl; mix well.
- Spoon crab meat mixture over tomato, piling 1 inch high. Place on baking sheet.
- Bake at 300 degrees for 30 to 40 minutes or until bubbly.

Alyce B. Squibb

Ham and Provolone Cheese Hot Sandwiches

3/4 cup butter, softened
1 1/2 teaspoons poppy
   seeds
1 1/2 teaspoons prepared
   mustard
1 1/2 teaspoons horseradish
2 teaspoons finely
   chopped onion
Worcestershire sauce to
   taste
Garlic salt to taste
8 Kaiser rolls, split
16 slices extra-smoky
   provolone cheese
16 slices ham

Yield: 8 servings

- Combine butter, poppy seeds, mustard, horseradish, onion, Worcestershire sauce and garlic salt in bowl; mix well.
- Spread cut sides of rolls with butter mixture. Layer cheese and ham on bottom half; top with remaining bread half.
- Wrap rolls in foil. Place on baking sheet.
- Bake at 350 degrees for 15 minutes.
- May microwave for 3 minutes. May freeze for future use; thaw before baking.

Rosemary E. Miller

Wheeling Hospital was chartered in 1850 by the Commonwealth of Virginia as a hospital and pest house (for those with infectious diseases). It was the first hospital in West Virginia. Wheeling Hospital continues to serve as a comprehensive health care facility with strong emphasis towards wellness.

Party Time Sloppy Joes

This is an old family recipe which is very popular with children.

2 pounds lean ground beef
1 onion, chopped
1 green bell pepper,
   chopped
2 cups catsup
1/4 cup packed brown
   sugar
1/4 cup prepared mustard
1 teaspoon Worcestershire
   sauce
1 (10-ounce) can tomato
   soup

Yield: 12 servings

• Brown ground beef with onion and green pepper in skillet, stirring until ground beef is crumbly; drain.
• Stir in catsup, brown sugar, mustard, Worcestershire sauce and soup.
• Simmer for 20 minutes, stirring occasionally.
• Serve on toasted buns.

Janet Kropp

Stromboli

May be served as an appetizer

2 loaves frozen bread
   dough, thawed
8 ounces sliced deli ham
16 ounces provolone
   cheese, thinly sliced
8 ounces sliced deli salami
8 ounces sliced pepperoni
1 egg, beaten
1 teaspoon olive oil
Italian seasoning to taste
Garlic salt to taste
1/2 cup grated Parmesan
   cheese

Yield: 24 servings

• Roll dough into two 10x15-inch rectangles on lightly floured surface.
• Place single layer of ham over dough; top with single layer of provolone cheese.
• Alternate layers of remaining ham, salami, pepperoni and remaining provolone cheese until all ingredients are used; roll to enclose filling.
• Place loaves seam side down on baking sheet. Brush with mixture of egg and olive oil. Sprinkle with Italian seasoning, garlic salt and Parmesan cheese.
• Bake at 375 degrees for 15 to 20 minutes or until brown.
• Let stand for 10 minutes before slicing. Serve with your favorite pizza sauce.

Sarah L. Gompers

Salads

Photo caption text visible in image: MAIL POUCH — PEOPLES FAVORITE. PRONOUNCED THE BEST. WHEELING - BENWOOD. WHEELING RAIL WAY CO.

W H E E L I N G

Wheeling Railway Company

The Wheeling Railway Company was organized in 1887 by John M. Sweeney, one of the founders of the Wheeling Electrical Company.

The first electric trolley began operating March 15, 1888. The maiden run of the electric trolley, according to a local newspaper account, went smoothly until the trolley began to cross the Main Street Bridge, at which time the front wheels jumped the track. Fortunately, one hundred hands were quick to put her back on track.

photograph courtesy of Gary Zearott, Zee Photo

Cranberry Mousse

1 (16-ounce) can crushed
  pineapple
1 (6-ounce) package
  strawberry gelatin
1 cup water
1 (16-ounce) can whole
  berry cranberry sauce
3 tablespoons lemon juice
1 teaspoon grated lemon
  rind
1/4 teaspoon nutmeg
2 cups sour cream
1/2 cup chopped pecans

Yield: 10 servings

- Drain pineapple, reserving juice.
- Bring gelatin, reserved juice and water to a
  boil in saucepan, stirring occasionally.
  Remove from heat.
- Stir in cranberry sauce, lemon juice, lemon
  rind and nutmeg. Chill until slightly
  thickened.
- Add sour cream, pineapple and pecans; mix
  well. Spoon into mold or 9x13-inch dish.
- Chill until set.

Cynthia L. Reasbeck

Cranberry and Orange Mold

2 (3-ounce) packages red
  raspberry gelatin
2 1/2 cups boiling water
1 (8-ounce) can crushed
  pineapple
1 (11-ounce) can
  mandarin oranges,
  drained
1 (12-ounce) jar
  cranberry-orange sauce
1/2 cup chopped pecans

Yield: 8 servings

- Dissolve gelatin in boiling water in bowl;
  mix well.
- Stir in undrained pineapple, mandarin
  oranges and cranberry-orange sauce. Add
  pecans; mix well.
- Pour into mold or 8x8-inch dish. Chill
  overnight.
- Serve with chicken or turkey.

Ann Bopp

Four Fruit Salad

3 medium bananas, sliced
Sections of 4 oranges
1 (16-ounce) can pitted
  dark sweet cherries,
  drained
1 cup seedless green
  grapes
1/2 cup sour cream
1 tablespoon honey
1 tablespoon orange juice

Yield: 10 servings

- Combine bananas, orange sections, cherries
  and grapes in bowl; mix well. Chill for 1
  hour.
- Combine sour cream, honey and orange
  juice in bowl; mix well.
- Toss fruit with sour cream mixture just
  before serving.

Pam Lacefield

Pretzel Salad

1 (6-ounce) package
  strawberry gelatin
1½ cups boiling water
2 cups frozen strawberries
1 (8-ounce) can crushed
  pineapple
1 cup crushed pretzels
⅓ cup melted butter
½ cup sugar
8 ounces cream cheese,
  softened
½ cup confectioners'
  sugar
8 ounces whipped topping

Yield: 10 servings

• Dissolve gelatin in boiling water in bowl; mix well. Stir in strawberries and undrained pineapple. Let stand until slightly thickened.
• Combine pretzels, melted butter and sugar in bowl; mix well. Press into 9x13-inch baking pan. Bake at 350 degrees for 12 minutes. Cool.
• Beat cream cheese, confectioners' sugar and whipped topping in mixer bowl until smooth. Spread over baked layer.
• Spread thickened gelatin mixture over cream cheese mixture.
• Chill until set.

Melissa Lucas Graham

Classic Waldorf Salad

Marjorie Klemm suggests adding chopped cooked chicken breasts and serving on a bed of lettuce.

½ cup whipping cream
¼ cup mayonnaise
1 tablespoon lemon juice
1 tablespoon sugar
2 cups chopped unpeeled
  apples
1 cup sliced celery
½ cup chopped walnuts

Yield: 4 servings

• Beat whipping cream in mixer bowl until soft peaks form. Chill.
• Combine mayonnaise, lemon juice and sugar in bowl; mix well. Stir in whipped cream gently.
• Fold in apples, celery and walnuts gently, tossing to coat.

Brenda G. Moore

Wheeling was designated a U.S. Port of Entry in 1831. It was stated in 1852 that importations came to the town by way of New Orleans, New York, Philadelphia, and Baltimore.

BAM Chicken Salad

2 cloves of garlic
1/2 cup vegetable oil
1/2 cup olive oil
1/4 cup lemon juice
1 cup grated Parmesan
  cheese
1 tablespoon
  Worcestershire sauce
1 teaspoon pepper
Salt to taste
5 tablespoons mayonnaise
2 to 4 chicken breast filets
Olive oil to taste
Pepper to taste
1 head romaine lettuce,
  torn
1/2 to 1 cup croutons

Yield: 8 servings

- Process garlic, vegetable oil, 1/2 cup olive oil, lemon juice, cheese, Worcestershire sauce, 1 teaspoon pepper and salt in blender until blended. Add mayonnaise. Process until creamy. Chill.
- Rinse chicken and pat dry. Brush with olive oil to taste. Season with salt and pepper to taste.
- Grill over hot coals for 20 minutes or until tender, turning once. Cut into thin strips.
- Arrange romaine on platter; top with chicken strips. Pour chilled dressing over chicken; sprinkle with croutons.

Bridget M. Weaver

Dilled Chicken Salad

6 tablespoons mayonnaise
2 teaspoons dillweed
1 teaspoon celery seeds
2 teaspoons red wine
  vinegar
Salt and pepper to taste
1 teaspoon sugar
2 cups chopped cooked
  white meat chicken
1/4 cup chopped celery

Yield: 6 servings

- Combine mayonnaise, dillweed, celery seeds, wine vinegar, salt, pepper and sugar in bowl; mix well.
- Stir in chicken and celery. Chill, covered, in refrigerator.
- Serve as sandwich spread or on bed of lettuce.

Mary Yanda

Stone and Thomas department store has been on the same site since it moved two years after it began business across Main Street in 1847. In 1850, the shops were lighted by gas in time for the Christmas shopping season. Wheeling was the 49th city in the nation to have a gas company, and it had the first chartered gas company in Virginia.

Shrimp and Artichoke Salad

This is a wonderful main dish salad!

1 large onion, thinly sliced
2 pounds shrimp, cooked,
  peeled
12 bay leaves
1 (16-ounce) can
  artichoke hearts,
  drained
1/2 cup vegetable oil
1/2 cup vinegar
1 tablespoon dry mustard
1 teaspoon salt
1 teaspoon pepper
1 tablespoon horseradish
1 (3-ounce) jar capers,
  drained

Yield: 10 servings

- Layer onion, shrimp, bay leaves and artichoke hearts alternately in bowl until all ingredients are used.
- Pour mixture of oil, vinegar, dry mustard, salt, pepper and horseradish over shrimp mixture. Top with capers.
- Marinate, covered, in refrigerator for 24 hours, tossing occasionally. Discard bay leaves.

Rosemary E. Miller

Garlic Shrimp Salad

6 cloves of garlic, minced
1 teaspoon safflower oil
1 1/2 to 2 pounds medium
  peeled shrimp
2 large tomatoes, peeled,
  chopped
2 medium cucumbers,
  peeled, chopped
3 green onions, chopped
1 (16-ounce) can
  artichoke hearts,
  drained
3 cloves of garlic, minced
1/4 cup safflower oil
1/3 cup lemon juice
1/2 teaspoon basil
1/4 teaspoon dillweed
Salt and pepper to taste
1 avocado, sliced

Yield: 6 servings

- Sauté 6 cloves of garlic in 1 teaspoon safflower oil in skillet. Add shrimp; mix well. Cook for 2 to 3 minutes or until shrimp turn pink, stirring constantly. Transfer shrimp to bowl. Combine tomatoes, cucumbers, green onions and artichoke hearts with shrimp; mix well.
- Combine 3 cloves of garlic, 1/4 cup safflower oil, lemon juice, basil, dillweed, salt and pepper in small bowl; mix well. Pour over shrimp mixture, tossing to coat shrimp and vegetables. Stir in avocado slices gently.
- Serve with French bread or pita bread.
- May substitute chicken for shrimp.

Hali Exley

Macaroni and Seafood Salad

1 (4-ounce) can small
   shrimp
10 hard-boiled eggs,
   chopped
1 medium onion, finely
   chopped
3 ribs celery, chopped
1 (16-ounce) package
   macaroni, cooked,
   drained
4 cups mayonnaise or to
   taste
1 (6-ounce) can tuna,
   drained, flaked
Salt to taste

Yield: 16 servings

- Drain shrimp, reserving 12 for topping; chop remaining shrimp. Combine eggs, onion, celery and macaroni in bowl; mix well. Stir in mayonnaise. Add tuna; mix well. Season with salt. Stir in chopped shrimp.
- Spoon into 4-quart serving bowl; top with reserved shrimp. Chill, covered, overnight to enhance flavor.

Cindy Richards

Seafood and Pasta Salad

An award winning recipe!

1 pound rotini, cooked,
   drained
1 pound peeled shrimp,
   cooked
1 cup broccoli flowerets,
   cooked tender-crisp
2 green bell peppers,
   chopped
2 tomatoes, cut into
   wedges
3 scallions, chopped
1 (6-ounce) can crab
   meat, drained, flaked
1/2 cup mayonnaise
1 (8-ounce) bottle of
   Italian salad dressing
1 1/2 tablespoons salad
   seasoning
3/4 cup grated Parmesan
   cheese

Yield: 8 servings

- Combine rotini, shrimp, broccoli, green peppers, tomatoes, scallions, crab meat, mayonnaise, salad dressing, salad seasoning and cheese in bowl; mix well.
- Chill, covered, for 4 hours.
- May store in refrigerator for up to 2 days. May add additional salad dressing if needed for desired consistency.

Susie Pere

Pasta Salad Jarlsberg

3 cups fusilli, cooked
1 cup chopped tomatoes
1 cup sliced salami, cut
  into strips
1 cup shredded Jarlsberg
  cheese
1/2 cup thinly sliced celery
1/2 cup chopped purple
  onion
1/2 cup chopped green bell
  pepper
1/3 cup sliced black olives
1/3 cup chopped pimentos
1/2 cup Italian salad
  dressing
2 tablespoons chopped
  fresh parsley
1 small clove of garlic,
  minced
1/2 teaspoon salt
1/4 teaspoon sugar
1/8 teaspoon ground pepper

Yield: 10 servings

- Combine fusilli, tomatoes, salami, cheese, celery, onion, green pepper, olives and pimentos in bowl; mix well.
- Mix Italian salad dressing, parsley, garlic, salt, sugar and pepper in bowl. Pour over pasta mixture, tossing to coat.
- Chill, covered, for several hours. Serve on a bed of lettuce.

Julie Squibb

Feta Cheese Pasta Salad

2 tablespoons lemon juice
1/2 cup vegetable oil
1/4 teaspoon pepper
1/4 teaspoon oregano
8 ounces rotini, cooked,
  drained
2 tomatoes, cut into
  wedges
1 small cucumber, peeled,
  sliced
1 cup chopped broccoli
1/2 cup sliced black olives
6 ounces feta cheese,
  crumbled
1/4 cup sliced green onions
2 tablespoons chopped
  fresh parsley

Yield: 8 servings

- Whisk lemon juice, oil, pepper and oregano in bowl until thick and creamy. Chill, covered, in refrigerator.
- Combine rotini, tomatoes, cucumber, broccoli, olives, feta cheese, green onions and parsley in bowl; mix well. Pour chilled dressing over rotini mixture, tossing to coat.
- May be prepared several days in advance and stored in refrigerator.

Pam Lacefield

Company Asparagus and Rice Salad

1 cup uncooked white rice
2 cups water
Salt to taste
12 ounces asparagus, cut
  into 1-inch diagonal
  slices
1/4 cup olive oil
1 teaspoon grated lemon
  rind
3 tablespoons lemon juice
1/2 teaspoon salt
1/4 teaspoon pepper
1/2 cup chopped green
  onions
1/4 cup grated Parmesan
  cheese
2 hard-boiled eggs,
  chopped

Yield: 6 servings

- Combine rice with water and salt in
  saucepan. Cook, covered, for 15 to 20
  minutes or until tender; remove cover. Let
  rice stand for 5 minutes; fluff with fork.
  Cool to room temperature.
- Steam asparagus in steamer for 3 minutes or
  until tender-crisp.
- Whisk olive oil, lemon rind, lemon juice,
  salt and pepper in large bowl until blended.
  Stir in rice, asparagus, green onions and
  cheese.
- Spoon into serving bowl; sprinkle with
  chopped eggs. Serve warm or at room
  temperature.

Carol Tyler

Wild Rice and Artichoke Salad

1 (6-ounce) package long
  grain and wild rice,
  cooked
1 (14-ounce) can
  artichoke hearts,
  drained, coarsely
  chopped
2 green onions, sliced
2 medium tomatoes,
  coarsely chopped
1/4 cup vegetable oil
2 tablespoons red wine
  vinegar
1 clove of garlic, minced

Yield: 6 servings

- Combine rice, artichokes and green onions
  in bowl; mix well. Chill, covered, in
  refrigerator.
- Combine tomatoes, oil, wine vinegar and
  garlic in saucepan; mix well. Cook until
  heated through, stirring constantly. Stir into
  rice mixture. Chill.

Kathy Neidhardt

The ladies of a church held a fund raiser dinner in 1854.
The charge was 50 cents for refreshments, which included such
items as oysters, ice cream and cakes.

Aunt Tina's Four Bean Salad

1 (16-ounce) can red
  kidney beans, drained
1 (16-ounce) can cut
  green beans, drained
1 (16-ounce) can cut wax
  beans, drained
1 (16-ounce) can garbanzo
  beans, drained
1 medium onion, finely
  chopped
3/4 cup sugar
2/3 cup vinegar
1 teaspoon salt
1/2 teaspoon pepper
1/2 cup vegetable oil

Yield: 6 servings

• Combine kidney beans, green beans, wax
  beans, garbanzo beans and onion in bowl;
  mix well.
• Whisk sugar, vinegar, salt, pepper and oil in
  bowl until blended. Pour over bean
  mixture, tossing to coat.
• Chill, covered, in refrigerator. Serve on bed
  of salad greens.

Kathy Neidhardt

White Bean Salad

The rosemary adds a wonderful flavor!

1 (16-ounce) can navy
  beans, drained
1 (2-ounce) jar pimento,
  drained, chopped
1 clove of garlic, minced
1/2 teaspoon pepper
1 tablespoon olive oil
2 tablespoons red wine
  vinegar
2 tablespoons capers
1/2 teaspoon rosemary

Yield: 6 servings

• Combine navy beans, pimento, garlic,
  pepper, olive oil, wine vinegar, capers and
  rosemary in bowl; mix well.
• Spoon onto lettuce-lined platter. Serve at
  room temperature.

Diana T. Ihlenfeld

*In 1856, the same year that the Christmas tree was introduced in the
White House, Wheeling also had a decorated tree in a church.
An 1860s Christmas tree to remember was made of gas pipes with over 200
jets of gas which made a brilliant spectacle. It was decorated
with evergreens, all types of toys, and taxidermic flying squirrels.*

Broccoli Salad

1 head broccoli, cut into
   bite-sized pieces
1/2 cup raisins
1 small red onion,
   chopped
8 slices crisp-fried bacon,
   crumbled
3/4 cup mayonnaise
1/2 cup sugar
2 teaspoons vinegar
Salt to taste
1/2 to 1 cup shredded
   Cheddar cheese

Yield: 6 servings

- Combine broccoli, raisins, red onion and
  bacon in bowl; mix well.
- Stir in mixture of mayonnaise, sugar,
  vinegar, salt and cheese.
- Chill, covered, for 2 hours.

Lori Dallas

Sesame Cabbage Salad

1 cup slivered almonds
2 tablespoons sesame
   seeds
1/2 cup vegetable oil
1 package
   chicken-flavored ramen
   noodles, broken
1 teaspoon salt
1 teaspoon pepper
2 tablespoons sugar
2 tablespoons cider
   vinegar
1/2 head cabbage, chopped
4 green onions, thinly
   sliced

Yield: 12 servings

- Sauté almonds and sesame seeds in oil in
  skillet.
- Combine ramen noodles and seasoning
  packet from noodles with salt, pepper, sugar
  and vinegar in bowl; mix well. Stir in
  almond mixture.
- Add cabbage and green onions; mix well.

Barbara Whitehead

The "Father of Oral Surgery," S. P. Hullihen, M.D., practiced in Wheeling.
He invented instruments and authored articles which were published
in medical journals worldwide. Following his death in 1857, a monument
was erected at his grave by the people of Wheeling. One of the
inscriptions states that they mourned his death as a "public calamity."

Cucumber Salad

1 cup chopped onion
1 cup chopped green bell
   pepper
2 cups sugar
1 cup vinegar
5 teaspoons salt
1 teaspoon celery salt
7 cups sliced cucumbers

Yield: 16 servings

- Combine onion, green pepper, sugar, vinegar, salt and celery salt in bowl; mix well.
- Pour over cucumbers in glass serving bowl; do not mix. Chill, covered, for 24 hours.

Beverly K. Smith

Bleu Cheese Potato Salad

Uptown potato salad!

3 pounds new potatoes,
   peeled, cut into
   quarters, cooked
3/4 teaspoon salt
1/4 teaspoon white pepper
2 tablespoons chopped
   fresh parsley
3 green onions, thinly
   sliced
3 hard-boiled eggs,
   chopped
1/3 cup slivered almonds,
   toasted
1 cup sour cream
2 tablespoons milk
1/4 teaspoon white wine
   vinegar
4 ounces bleu cheese,
   crumbled
1 head radicchio,
   separated into leaves
4 slices crisp-fried bacon,
   crumbled
Parsley sprigs

Yield: 10 servings

- Combine potatoes, salt, white pepper, chopped parsley, green onions, eggs and almonds in bowl; mix well.
- Combine sour cream, milk, wine vinegar and bleu cheese in bowl; mix well. Stir into potato mixture.
- Chill, covered, for 2 hours or longer.
- Spoon potato salad into radicchio-lined serving bowl; sprinkle with bacon. Top with parsley sprigs.

Lori Dallas

Dilled Potato Salad

1/2 cup mayonnaise
1/4 cup sour cream
2 teaspoons dillweed
2 teaspoons white or cider
  vinegar
1 teaspoon sugar
Salt to taste
11/2 pounds red potatoes,
  cooked, cut into
  quarters, chilled
1/2 cup chopped dill
  pickles

Yield: 8 servings

- Combine mayonnaise, sour cream, dillweed, vinegar, sugar and salt in bowl; mix well.
- Combine mayonnaise mixture with potatoes in bowl. Stir in dill pickles gently.

Mary Yanda

German Potato Salad

Passed down through generations

4 slices bacon, chopped
1/4 cup chopped onion
1/2 cup vinegar
1/4 cup water
1/2 teaspoon sugar
8 medium potatoes,
  cooked, peeled, chopped
Salt to taste
2 hard-boiled eggs,
  chopped
1 hard-boiled egg, sliced

Yield: 8 servings

- Fry bacon in skillet until crisp. Drain, reserving pan drippings.
- Sauté onion in pan drippings. Stir in mixture of vinegar, water and sugar.
- Combine bacon and warm potatoes in bowl; mix well. Pour vinegar mixture over potatoes; season with salt.
- Let stand at room temperature for several hours. Stir in chopped eggs; top with sliced egg.

Rosemary E. Miller

A five-inch to six-inch snowfall in December of 1859 led to "100 children snowballing on the corner of 12th and Market Streets and sleigh rides on the National Road." Later in the month "2,000 men and boys" were out sliding on city streets with their sleds speeding "100 miles an hour at least."

Heart Smart Potato Salad

4 pounds red potatoes
  with skins, cooked,
  chopped
8 hard-boiled egg whites
2 cups chopped celery
1 cup grated carrots
1 cup chopped green
  onions
1 cup chopped red bell
  pepper
1/2 cup chopped fresh
  parsley
1 cup nonfat plain yogurt
1/2 cup light mayonnaise
1 teaspoon mustard
2 drops of Tabasco sauce
2 teaspoons
  Worcestershire sauce
2 teaspoons celery seeds
1/2 teaspoon garlic powder
1/8 teaspoon white pepper
1 teaspoon paprika

Yield: 8 servings

- Combine potatoes, egg whites, celery, carrots, green onions, bell pepper and parsley in bowl; mix well.
- Combine yogurt, mayonnaise, mustard, Tabasco sauce, Worcestershire sauce, celery seeds, garlic powder, white pepper and paprika in bowl; mix well.
- Stir yogurt mixture into potato mixture.

Jan Berardinelli

Marinated Vegetable Salad

1 medium zucchini,
  chopped
2 medium carrots, sliced
8 cherry tomatoes, cut
  into halves
6 packages frozen pea
  pods, thawed, drained
2 medium tomatoes,
  chopped
1 onion, sliced into rings
1/4 cup olive oil
1/2 cup white wine vinegar
  or tarragon vinegar
1/4 cup sugar
1/4 teaspoon dry mustard
3/4 teaspoon seasoned salt
1/2 teaspoon freshly
  ground pepper

Yield: 16 servings

- Combine zucchini, carrots, cherry tomatoes, pea pods, tomatoes and onion in large bowl.
- Combine olive oil, wine vinegar, sugar, dry mustard, seasoned salt and pepper in airtight container; shake to mix well. Pour over vegetables.
- Marinate, covered, in refrigerator for 1 hour to overnight. Serve in lettuce cups.

Samantha Hensel Buch

Citrus Salad with Lime Vinaigrette

2 tablespoons lime juice
Salt to taste
2 teaspoons honey
2 teaspoons rice vinegar
Ginger to taste
Cayenne pepper to taste
2 teaspoons canola oil
1 cup torn Boston lettuce
1 cup torn Bibb lettuce
1 cup torn red leaf lettuce
1 cup torn romaine lettuce
Sections of 1 orange
Sections of 1 grapefruit
1/4 red onion, thinly
    sliced, separated into
    rings

Yield: 4 servings

• Combine lime juice, salt, honey, rice
  vinegar, ginger, cayenne pepper and canola
  oil in covered container, shaking to mix.
  Chill.
• Arrange 1 cup mixed lettuce on salad plate.
  Top with 4 orange sections, 4 grapefruit
  sections and onion rings; drizzle with
  chilled dressing. Repeat process until all
  ingredients are used.

Hali Exley

Winter Layer Salad

1/2 head lettuce, torn into
    bite-sized pieces
2 cups sliced celery
1 Bermuda red onion,
    thinly sliced
2 cucumbers, thinly sliced
1 1/2 cups sour cream
2 tablespoons sugar
1 cup mayonnaise
1 1/2 tablespoons vinegar
Pepper to taste
1 pound bacon,
    crisp-fried, crumbled
1 cup grated Parmesan
    cheese

Yield: 12 servings

• Layer lettuce, celery, red onion and
  cucumbers in order listed in 9x13-inch dish.
• Spread mixture of sour cream and sugar
  over cucumbers. Top with mixture of
  mayonnaise, vinegar and pepper.
• Sprinkle with bacon and cheese.
• Chill, covered, overnight.

Rosemary E. Miller

*It was recommended in 1859 that sanitary precautions be taken
during the summer. Nothing offensive should remain indoors such as liquid
in which vegetables are cooked as they "emit a most unpleasant
and unwholesome smell." Every room should be swept and dusted daily,
including cleansing under the beds, drawers, and tables.*

Romaine and Orange Salad

A company favorite!

1/2 head iceberg lettuce, torn
1/2 head romaine lettuce, torn
1/2 cup chopped celery
4 green onions, sliced
1/2 cup vegetable oil
2 tablespoons sugar
2 tablespoons parsley
1 teaspoon salt
1/4 cup vinegar
Pepper to taste
1/4 cup sliced almonds
1 1/2 tablespoons sugar
1 (11-ounce) can mandarin oranges, drained

Yield: 6 servings

- Combine iceberg lettuce, romaine lettuce, celery and green onions in bowl; mix well. Chill, covered, in refrigerator.
- Combine oil, sugar, parsley, salt, vinegar and pepper in covered container, shaking to mix. Chill for 1 hour or longer.
- Combine almonds and sugar in skillet; mix well. Cook over low heat until sugar melts and almonds are brown, stirring constantly. Cool.
- Stir mandarin oranges into chilled lettuce mixture; drizzle with dressing. Sprinkle with almonds just before serving.
- May substitute bottled sweet and sour dressing for homemade dressing.

Maureen Barte

Roquefort Salad

May be prepared 3 days in advance

3/4 cup mayonnaise
1/2 cup vegetable oil
1 tablespoon white or cider vinegar
2 teaspoons sugar
1 teaspoon parsley flakes
1/4 teaspoon garlic powder
1/2 teaspoon ground pepper
6 ounces Roquefort cheese, crumbled
2 tablespoons grated Parmesan cheese
6 cups torn romaine lettuce leaves
3/4 cup black olives
1/2 cup chopped scallions
3/4 cup seasoned croutons

Yield: 6 servings

- Whisk mayonnaise, oil, vinegar and sugar in bowl. Stir in parsley, garlic powder and pepper. Add Roquefort cheese; mix well. Fold in Parmesan cheese.
- Arrange mixture of lettuce, olives and scallions on salad plates. Drizzle with dressing; sprinkle with croutons.

Mary Yanda

Indian Spinach Salad

1/4 cup white wine vinegar
1/2 cup vegetable oil
2 tablespoons chutney,
  chopped
2 teaspoons sugar
1/2 teaspoon salt
1 1/2 teaspoons curry
  powder
1 teaspoon dry mustard
10 ounces spinach, torn
  into bite-sized pieces
1 1/2 cups chopped
  unpeeled apples
1/2 cup raisins
1/2 cup salted peanuts
2 tablespoons sliced green
  onions

Yield: 8 servings

• Combine wine vinegar, oil, chutney, sugar, salt, curry powder and dry mustard in covered container, shaking to mix. Chill.
• Arrange spinach in large salad bowl. Top with apples, raisins, peanuts and green onions.
• Pour dressing over spinach mixture, tossing to mix well.

Beverly B. Fluty

French Dressing

1 small clove of garlic,
  crushed
1/2 cup corn oil
1/4 cup white wine vinegar
1 teaspoon salt
1/2 teaspoon pepper
1/2 teaspoon dry mustard

Yield: 6 servings

• Combine garlic, corn oil, wine vinegar, salt, pepper and dry mustard in covered container, shaking to mix.

Roanne M. Burech

The Virginia State Republican Convention met at Wheeling on May 2, 1860. Even the rolling mills suspended operations in order that the employees might attend the session. One order of business was the appointment of delegates to the National Convention at Chicago on May 16. It was there that Abraham Lincoln was nominated for President of the United States.

Poppy Seed Salad Dressing

1/2 cup sugar
1 tablespoon sesame seeds
1 tablespoon poppy seeds
1 1/2 teaspoons minced
   onion
1/4 teaspoon paprika
1/4 teaspoon
   Worcestershire sauce
1/4 cup raspberry or cider
   vinegar
1/2 cup vegetable oil

Yield: 8 servings

- Combine sugar, sesame seeds, poppy seeds, onion, paprika, Worcestershire sauce and raspberry vinegar in blender container; process until smooth.
- Add oil gradually, processing constantly until thick and smooth.

Kathy Tannenbaum

Tangy Vinaigrette

1/2 cup olive oil
3 tablespoons orange juice
3 tablespoons white wine
   vinegar or tarragon
   vinegar
2 tablespoons sliced
   almonds
1 tablespoon chopped
   pimento
3/4 teaspoon chopped
   cilantro or parsley
1/2 teaspoon salt
1/4 teaspoon freshly
   ground pepper

Yield: 12 servings

- Combine olive oil, orange juice, wine vinegar, almonds, pimento, cilantro, salt and pepper in airtight container; mix well. Chill until serving time.
- Serve over salad of greens, mandarin oranges and apples.

Samantha Hensel Buch

On New Year's Eve, 1862, President Abraham Lincoln signed the bill granting West Virginia statehood. Wheeling is the only city in the country to have served as the capital of two state governments.

Entrées

W H E E L I N G

Mount de Chantal Visitation Academy

In 1848, eight Visitation sisters came to the frontier at the request of Bishop Whelan to establish an independent school for girls of all faiths. Five days after their arrival, the sisters opened the academy in downtown Wheeling, thus making Mount de Chantal Visitation Academy older than the state of West Virginia.

The Steenrod farm was purchased in 1860. On this land, the new convent and academy was to "provide ample space to afford an inexhaustible supply of fresh air, and full scope for outdoor exercise." Plans were drawn up for the academy building, but as soon as the architect was entrusted with the necessary funds, he absconded with both the funds and the plans. The present Mount de Chantal Academy building was built in 1865. The more than one hundred acres surrounding the new complex contained orchards, gardens, and pasture land as well as recreational areas for the students. The edifice itself extended two hundred fifty feet and was constructed of bricks made on the site with a foundation of native sandstone. Bishop Whelan is known to have set many a brick in place himself. Mount de Chantal Visitation Academy is listed on the National Register of Historic Places.

Mount de Chantal Visitation Academy remains a leader in college preparatory education.

photograph courtesy of Mount de Chantal Archives

London Broil

1/2 cup wine vinegar
1/4 cup catsup
2 tablespoons vegetable oil
2 tablespoons soy sauce
1 tablespoon
  Worcestershire sauce
1 tablespoon prepared
  mustard
1/4 teaspoon garlic powder
1 teaspoon salt
1/4 teaspoon pepper
1 (3-pound) London broil

Yield: 10 servings

- Combine vinegar, catsup, oil, soy sauce, Worcestershire sauce, mustard, garlic powder, salt and pepper in shallow dish; mix well.
- Add London broil, coating well. Marinate in refrigerator for several hours to overnight.
- Grill for 35 to 40 minutes or until done to taste. May substitute chuck roast for London broil.

Gretchen Courtney Hooper

Wine Baked Beef

This is an excellent make-ahead recipe—perfect for company.

3 large shallots, minced
1 large clove of garlic,
  minced
2 tablespoons butter
1 cup Madeira
1 cup beef broth
2 teaspoons cornstarch
2 tablespoons red wine
2 dashes of browning
  sauce
Salt and freshly ground
  pepper to taste
1 (4-pound) beef
  tenderloin
1 clove of garlic, cut into
  halves
2 tablespoons butter
2 tablespoons vegetable oil

Yield: 12 servings

- Sauté shallots and minced garlic in 2 tablespoons butter in large skillet until tender but not brown. Add Madeira and 3/4 cup beef broth. Simmer until liquid is reduced to 1 cup.
- Whisk in mixture of cornstarch and remaining 1/4 cup beef broth. Cook over medium heat for 5 minutes or until thickened, whisking constantly.
- Stir in red wine, browning sauce and salt and pepper. Strain into bowl; set aside.
- Cut beef into 2 or 3 pieces. Rub with garlic halves, sprinkle with salt and pepper. Sear for 2 to 3 minutes on each side in heated mixture of 2 tablespoons butter and oil in Dutch oven over high heat. Add strained sauce. Cool slightly. Slice into serving portions. Arrange in single layer in ovenproof dish. May refrigerate, covered, at this point.
- Bring to room temperature. Bake, covered, at 350 degrees for 15 minutes. Bake, uncovered, for 5 minutes longer.

Miriam King

2

Matambre with Chili Sauce

2 (2-pound) flank steaks,
  butterflied
1 cup thawed frozen
  mixed vegetables
1/2 cup finely chopped
  onion
1/4 cup finely chopped
  green bell pepper
1/4 cup finely chopped
  pimento
2 teaspoons finely minced
  chili pepper
1 clove of garlic, crushed
1 teaspoon salt
2 cups (about) beef broth
1 rib celery, sliced
1 carrot, sliced
1 onion, sliced
1 clove of garlic, chopped
Chili Sauce

Yield: 8 servings

- Trim sides of steaks straight. Pound each
  steak into 12x12-inch rectangle. Arrange
  side by side, overlapping edges 1 inch or
  more.
- Combine mixed vegetables, chopped onion,
  green pepper, pimento, chili pepper,
  crushed garlic and salt in bowl; mix well.
  Spread over steaks. Roll up steaks as tightly
  as possible to enclose filling; tie every 3
  inches.
- Place in shallow baking dish. Add beef
  broth, celery, carrot, sliced onion and 1
  clove of garlic.
- Bake, covered, at 350 degrees for 2 hours,
  basting several times. Remove to platter; let
  rest for 15 minutes. Slice carefully with
  sharp knife. Serve with Chili Sauce.

Chili Sauce

1 onion, finely chopped
1 green bell pepper, finely
  chopped
1 clove of garlic, minced
1/4 cup butter
2 tablespoons flour
1 tablespoon chili powder
1 teaspoon salt
Freshly ground pepper to
  taste
1 cup tomato juice
1 cup beef broth

Yield: 8 servings

- Sauté onion, green pepper and garlic in
  butter in medium skillet for 5 minutes or
  until tender but not brown.
- Stir in flour, chili powder, salt and pepper.
  Cook over low heat for 2 minutes. Stir in
  tomato juice and beef broth. Cook over
  medium heat until slightly thickened,
  stirring constantly. Serve hot.

Marilyn Grist

*In 1860, a public hanging was considered a source
of family entertainment.*

Beef Bourguignon

3 pounds stew beef,
   trimmed, cut into
   1-inch cubes
1 recipe Marinade for Beef
   Bourguignon
2 tablespoons vegetable oil
Salt and freshly ground
   pepper to taste
2 tablespoons flour
1/4 cup vegetable oil
2 cups red wine
2 tablespoons tomato
   paste
1 tablespoon flour
1 cup beef consommé

Yield: 10 servings

- Combine beef with marinade in glass bowl, covering completely; sprinkle with 2 tablespoons oil. Marinate, covered, in refrigerator overnight. Drain, discarding marinade. Drain beef and vegetables on paper towels.
- Sprinkle beef cubes with salt and pepper; coat with 2 tablespoons flour. Brown in 1/4 cup heated oil in skillet; remove to slow cooker with slotted spoon.
- Add vegetables from marinade to skillet. Sauté until tender; remove to slow cooker. Add wine and tomato paste. Stir in mixture of 1 tablespoon flour and consommé; liquid should cover beef.
- Cook on Low for 3 to 4 hours or until very tender. Serve in large bowls with French bread.
- May cook in electric skillet at 375 degrees for 2½ hours if preferred.

Marinade for Beef Bourguignon

2 cloves of garlic, crushed
1 onion, sliced
1 carrot, sliced
6 ounces mushrooms,
   sliced
5 sprigs of parsley
10 peppercorns, crushed
2 tablespoons French
   salad dressing
1/4 cup brandy
1 cup Burgundy
1/4 teaspoon thyme
1 teaspoon salt

Yield: 10 servings

- Combine garlic, onion, carrot, mushrooms, parsley, peppercorns, salad dressing, brandy, wine, thyme and salt in bowl; mix well.

Kathy Tannenbaum

*Several people were arrested in 1862 for purchasing goods at
the Centre Market before the bell rang for the opening.*

Foolproof Beef and Broccoli

1 pound boneless sirloin
  steak
1 clove of garlic, minced
1 teaspoon vegetable oil
1 medium onion, cut into
  wedges
1 (10-ounce) can cream of
  broccoli soup
1/4 cup water
1 teaspoon soy sauce
2 cups broccoli flowerets

Yield: 4 servings

- Slice beef cross grain into thin strips. Sauté with garlic in hot oil in skillet over medium-high heat until brown. Add onion. Sauté for 5 minutes, stirring frequently.
- Stir in soup, water and soy sauce. Bring to a boil. Add broccoli; reduce heat to low.
- Simmer, covered, for 5 minutes or until vegetables are tender. Serve over hot cooked noodles.

Debbie Wolfe

Beef and Artichoke Stew

2 onions, sliced
2 cloves of garlic, minced
3 tablespoons vegetable oil
2 1/2 pounds stew beef, cut
  into 1 1/2-inch cubes
1/3 cup flour
1 teaspoon salt
1/2 teaspoon pepper
1 teaspoon dillweed
1 cup Burgundy
1 (10-ounce) can beef
  consommé
1 (9-ounce) package
  frozen artichoke hearts
15 fresh mushrooms, cut
  into halves or quarters
3 tablespoons butter

Yield: 6 servings

- Sauté onions and garlic in heated oil in heavy saucepan; remove with slotted spoon.
- Coat beef with mixture of flour, salt and pepper. Brown in drippings in saucepan. Add garlic and onion mixture, dillweed, wine and consommé. Simmer for 1 1/2 to 2 hours or until beef is tender.
- Cook artichokes using package directions, reducing cooking time by 1 to 2 minutes. Sauté mushrooms in butter in skillet for 5 minutes. Add artichokes and mushrooms to stew. Adjust seasonings. Cook until heated through.
- May place in baking dish, top with canned biscuits and bake at 400 degrees for 10 to 15 minutes; brush with margarine, sprinkle with Parmesan cheese and bake for 5 minutes longer.

Carol Tyler

Beef Stew

2 pounds stew beef
30 to 40 ounces tomato
 juice
6 carrots, sliced
3 medium potatoes,
 peeled, sliced
1/2 cup chopped celery
2 small onions, chopped
1 slice bread, torn
1/2 cup water
1/2 cup red wine
3 tablespoons
 quick-cooking tapioca
1 tablespoon sugar
1 1/2 teaspoons salt

Yield: 8 servings

- Combine stew beef, tomato juice, carrots, potatoes, celery, onions, bread, water, wine, tapioca, sugar and salt in large bowl; mix well.
- Spoon into 3-quart baking dish. Bake, covered, at 350 degrees for 3 1/2 to 4 hours or until very tender.
- May substitute stewed tomatoes for tomato juice.

Alyce B. Squibb

Favorite Irish Stew

10 bay leaves
3/4 cup extra-virgin olive
 oil
6 pounds thick-cut round
 steak, cut into 1-inch
 cubes
6 large yellow onions,
 chopped
12 cloves of garlic, minced
2 tablespoons each
 rosemary and thyme
1 cup flour
12 1/2 cups beef stock
24 ounces Guiness extra
 stout
1 1/2 pounds carrots, sliced
1 1/2 pounds potatoes,
 sliced
Salt and pepper to taste

Yield: 30 servings

- Sauté bay leaves lightly in heated olive oil in 12-quart stockpot. Add steak. Cook over high heat until brown, stirring frequently.
- Add onions. Cook until onions are clear. Stir in garlic, rosemary, thyme and flour. Cook for several minutes, stirring until smooth.
- Add beef stock and stout. Simmer until thickened to desired consistency. Add carrots, potatoes, salt and pepper. Cook until vegetables are tender.
- Cool to room temperature. Chill overnight. Remove from refrigerator 1 or 2 hours before serving time. Simmer over low heat until heated through, stirring frequently. Discard bay leaves.

Laura Phillips Miller

Beef Stroganoff

2¹/2 to 3 pounds round or
  sirloin steak, cut into
  strips
¹/4 cup flour
Salt to taste
3 tablespoons margarine
1 medium onion, chopped
1 clove of garlic, minced
1 pound fresh
  mushrooms, sliced
2 cubes beef bouillon
20 ounces boiling water
1¹/2 tablespoons
  Worcestershire sauce
2 cups sour cream

Yield: 8 servings

- Coat steak with mixture of flour and salt.
  Brown in margarine in saucepan.
- Add onion, garlic and mushrooms. Sauté
  until tender-crisp. Stir in beef bouillon
  dissolved in water; add Worcestershire
  sauce.
- Simmer, covered, for 2 hours. Stir in sour
  cream. Simmer just until heated through.
  Serve over hot cooked noodles or rice.

Julie Squibb

Sukiyaki

This looks dreadful but tastes wonderful. Give it a try.

1 pound round steak
3 tablespoons olive oil
2 medium onions, sliced
12 green onions, sliced
6 stalks celery, sliced
8 ounces spinach, chopped
1 (7-ounce) can bamboo
  shoots, drained
¹/2 cup beef consommé
¹/4 cup soy sauce
1 tablespoon sugar
1 (7-ounce) can water
  chestnuts, drained

Yield: 6 servings

- Cut steak cross grain into very thin strips.
  Sauté in heated olive oil in skillet.
- Add onions, green onions, celery, spinach
  and bamboo shoots. Cook, covered, for 5
  minutes, stirring frequently.
- Add beef consommé, soy sauce, sugar and
  water chestnuts. Cook over low heat for 15
  minutes or until vegetables are tender.

Beverly B. Fluty

*The fashionable hoop skirts of the 1860s were
declared to be a public nuisance.*

Jalapeño and Beer Baked Short Ribs

2¼ cups canned tomato
   sauce
¼ cup red wine vinegar
¼ cup finely chopped
   jalapeño peppers
3 tablespoons chopped
   green bell pepper
¼ cup packed light
   brown sugar
1 tablespoon dry mustard
4 large cloves of garlic,
   minced
¼ teaspoon cinnamon
¼ teaspoon ground cloves
½ teaspoon cayenne
   pepper
2 cups beer
8 pounds beef short ribs,
   cut into 3-inch pieces
2 large onions, coarsely
   chopped

Yield: 8 servings

- Combine tomato sauce, vinegar, jalapeño peppers, green pepper, brown sugar, dry mustard, garlic, cinnamon, cloves and cayenne pepper in saucepan. Simmer for 10 minutes or until slightly thickened. Cool slightly. Stir in beer.
- Arrange short ribs in single layer in 2 large baking pans. Sprinkle onions around ribs. Spoon pepper mixture over ribs.
- Bake, covered with foil, at 425 degrees for 2½ hours or until ribs are tender.
- May prepare the day before and chill overnight. Skim surface of sauce and reheat at 375 degrees for 45 minutes.

Linda Holmstrand

Kefta

This is an authentic Lebanese dish.

1½ pounds ground chuck
1 onion, chopped
1 small bunch parsley,
   finely chopped
1 teaspoon salt
1 teaspoon oregano
¼ teaspoon cinnamon
¼ teaspoon pepper
1 tablespoon vegetable oil
3 tablespoons tomato
   paste

Yield: 6 servings

- Combine ground chuck, onion, parsley, salt, oregano, cinnamon and pepper in bowl; mix well. Shape into slightly flattened meatballs
- Brown in oil in large skillet; drain. Add tomato paste and enough water to cover.
- Bring to a boil; reduce heat. Simmer, covered, for 1 hour. Serve with mashed potatoes or rice.

Angela Nagem

Mexican Lasagna

1 pound ground beef
1 (12-ounce) jar thick and
   chunky salsa
6 flour tortillas
1 cup refried beans
1 cup sour cream
1 cup shredded Cheddar
   cheese

Yield: 6 servings

- Brown ground beef in skillet, stirring until crumbly. Stir in ¹/₂ cup of the salsa.
- Spread ¹/₄ cup of the salsa in shallow 10-inch baking dish. Arrange 2 tortillas in salsa. Layer beans, ground beef, sour cream, cheese and remaining tortillas ¹/₂ at a time in prepared dish.
- Bake, covered with foil, at 350 degrees for 30 minutes. Garnish with shredded lettuce, chopped tomatoes and additional sour cream. Serve with heated remaining salsa.

Caryn Buch

Ground Beef Stroganoff

2 pounds ground beef
2 medium onions, chopped
1 (4-ounce) can
   mushrooms
1 cup beef bouillon
3 tablespoons tomato
   paste
1¹/₂ teaspoons salt
¹/₄ teaspoon pepper
1 cup sour cream
2 tablespoons flour

Yield: 8 servings

- Brown ground beef in large skillet, stirring until crumbly. Add onions and mushrooms. Sauté until onions are golden brown; drain.
- Combine mixture with beef bouillon, tomato paste, salt and pepper in slow cooker; mix well. Cook on Low for 6 to 8 hours.
- Stir in mixture of sour cream and flour. Cook for 1 hour longer. Serve over hot cooked buttered noodles or rice.

Brenda K. Danehart

The horse-drawn cars of the street railway began operating in 1867.
Some of the horses were unaccustomed to pulling people in
cars which ran on iron tracks. One horse refused to move and lay
down several times on the route.

Swedish Meatballs

1¹/₂ cups soft bread
   crumbs
³/₄ cup milk
3 tablespoons finely
   chopped onion
2 tablespoons butter
1 pound ground chuck
1 egg, slightly beaten
¹/₄ teaspoon nutmeg
¹/₈ teaspoon pepper
¹/₄ cup flour
2 tablespoons butter
¹/₂ cup beef stock
¹/₂ cup whipping cream
1 to 1¹/₂ tablespoons flour

Yield: 6 servings

- Soak bread crumbs in milk in bowl. Sauté onion in 2 tablespoons butter in skillet. Add to bread crumbs with ground chuck, egg, nutmeg and pepper; mix well. Shape into 1-inch meatballs; coat with ¹/₄ cup flour.
- Sauté in 2 tablespoons butter in skillet for 10 minutes or until light brown. Add beef stock and cream. Simmer, covered, for 5 minutes. Remove meatballs to serving bowl with slotted spoon.
- Blend 1 to 1¹/₂ tablespoons flour with an equal amount of water in small bowl. Stir into cooking juices in skillet. Cook until thickened, stirring constantly. Spoon over meatballs.

Doretta Jacob

Beefy Zucchini Casserole

1 pound ground round
1 or 2 zucchini, sliced
3 tomatoes, chopped
1 green bell pepper,
   chopped
1 medium onion, chopped
1 (10-ounce) can tomato
   soup
1 teaspoon oregano
1 teaspoon basil
1 cup shredded
   mozzarella cheese
6 slices white bread, cubed
¹/₂ cup melted margarine
1 teaspoon oregano
1 teaspoon basil

Yield: 8 servings

- Brown ground round in large skillet, stirring until crumbly; drain. Add zucchini, tomatoes, green pepper, onion, tomato soup, 1 teaspoon oregano and 1 teaspoon basil; mix well.
- Cook over medium heat until vegetables are tender-crisp. Spoon into 9x13-inch baking dish; sprinkle with cheese.
- Toss bread cubes with melted margarine, 1 teaspoon oregano and 1 teaspoon basil in bowl. Sprinkle over casserole.
- Bake at 350 degrees for 30 minutes or until casserole is heated through and topping is golden brown.

Sarah L. Gompers

Elegant Veal Stew

3 medium onions, sliced
3 cloves of garlic, crushed
7 tablespoons olive oil
3 pounds veal stew meat, cubed
1/4 cup flour
2 (14-ounce) cans beef broth
3/4 cup white wine
Juice of 1 lemon
1 bay leaf
3/4 teaspoon rosemary
1/4 teaspoon thyme
1/8 teaspoon freshly ground pepper
2 (9-ounce) packages frozen artichoke hearts, partly thawed
1 pound fresh mushrooms, sliced
Grated rind of 1 lemon
1/4 cup chopped parsley
1/2 cup pitted black olives
1/4 cup pimento strips

Yield: 8 servings

- Sauté onions and garlic in 2 tablespoons olive oil in large skillet until clear. Remove to heavy 5-quart saucepan.
- Add 3 tablespoons olive oil to skillet. Cook veal in oil a few pieces at a time, removing pieces to saucepan as they brown.
- Add remaining 2 tablespoons oil and flour to skillet. Cook until smooth, stirring constantly. Add beef broth, wine and lemon juice, stirring to deglaze skillet. Add bay leaf, rosemary, thyme and pepper; mix well.
- Bring to a boil. Cook for 5 minutes. Pour over veal mixture in saucepan. Simmer, covered, for 1 hour. Simmer, uncovered, for 45 minutes longer, stirring frequently.
- Stir in artichokes. Cook for 15 minutes or until stew is of desired consistency.
- Cook mushrooms, covered, in skillet over high heat for 3 minutes. Cook, uncovered, until liquid has evaporated. Add to stew with remaining ingredients; mix well. Cook until heated through; discard bay leaf.

Beth Ann Dague

German Vinegar Ham and Beans

This recipe reflects Wheeling's German immigrant heritage.

2 pounds ham
1 ham hock
3 quarts water
2 pounds fresh green beans, broken into 1 1/2-inch pieces
6 medium potatoes, cut into halves
1/2 cup flour
1/2 cup vinegar

Yield: 8 servings

- Combine ham and ham hock with 3 quarts water in large saucepan. Cook for 2 hours. Add beans. Cook for 30 minutes. Add potatoes. Cook for 30 minutes. Remove ham and potatoes to large serving bowl.
- Blend flour and vinegar with enough water to make a paste. Stir in beans. Cook for 5 minutes or until thickened, stirring constantly. Serve with ham and potatoes.

Sarah S. Miller

Ham Loaf with Raisin Sauce

"Rave reviews from travelers with Harvey Show Tours."

2 pounds ground ham
1/4 pound ground pork
1 egg
1/2 cup packed brown
  sugar
1 (8-ounce) can crushed
  pineapple, drained
1 teaspoon ground cloves
1 teaspoon salt
1 tablespoon butter
1 tablespoon cornstarch
2 tablespoons lemon juice
1/2 cup sugar
1/2 cup packed brown
  sugar
1 3/4 cups water
1/2 cup raisins
1 teaspoon vanilla extract

Yield: 8 servings

- Combine ground ham, ground pork, egg, 1/2 cup brown sugar, pineapple, cloves and salt in bowl; mix well. Shape into loaf.
- Place in 4x8-inch loaf pan. Bake at 325 degrees for 1 1/2 hours.
- Combine butter, cornstarch, lemon juice, sugar, 1/2 cup brown sugar, water and raisins in saucepan. Cook until thickened, stirring constantly. Stir in vanilla.
- Remove meat loaf to serving plate. Spoon some of the raisin sauce over loaf. Serve with remaining raisin sauce.

Caryn Buch

Miniature Ham Loaves

3 cups ground cooked ham
1 egg, beaten
3/4 cup soft bread crumbs
1/4 cup milk
2 tablespoons finely
  chopped celery
2 tablespoons finely
  chopped onion
1/8 teaspoon dry mustard
Pepper to taste
1 tablespoon cornstarch
1/4 cup water
1/2 cup pineapple
  preserves

Yield: 4 servings

- Combine ground ham, egg, bread crumbs, milk, celery, onion, dry mustard and pepper in large bowl; mix well. Shape into 2 small loaves.
- Place loaves in shall baking pan. Bake at 350 degrees for 45 minutes.
- Blend cornstarch and water in small saucepan. Cook over medium-high heat for 2 minutes or until thickened, stirring constantly. Stir in preserves. Cook for 1 minute longer, stirring constantly.
- Remove ham loaves to serving plates; spoon pineapple sauce over loaves.

Debbie Wolfe

Grilled Pork Tenderloin

1 (8-ounce) bottle of
  Italian salad dressing
2 teaspoons rosemary
2 (1-pound) pork
  tenderloins

Yield: 6 servings

- Mix salad dressing and rosemary in shallow bowl. Add pork, coating well. Marinate in refrigerator for 6 to 8 hours; drain.
- Grill over hot coals for 15 to 20 minutes or until done to taste.

Diana T. Ihlenfeld

Roasted Pork Loin with Garlic

1 (3-pound) pork loin
3 cloves of garlic, slivered
Salt and freshly ground
  pepper to taste
1 tablespoon vegetable oil

Yield: 6 servings

- Cut deep slits in pork with small sharp knife. Place garlic slivers into slits. Sprinkle with salt and pepper.
- Brown on all sides in heated oil in small roasting pan over medium-high heat for 5 minutes. Insert meat thermometer.
- Roast at 425 degrees for 50 minutes or to 150 degrees on meat thermometer. Place on carving board; let stand for 10 minutes. Cut into 1/2-inch slices.

Ellen F. Sohn

The Soldiers and Sailors Monument in Wheeling Park was paid for by funds raised at the Sanitary Fair during the Civil War. It was first situated at the City-County Building in 1883. When that building was razed in 1956, the monument was moved to a new location. It was moved two more times. After the second move, the positions of the soldier and sailor were reversed when the monument was reassembled.

Pork Chops with Apples

6 thick pork chops or
  butterflied pork loin
  chops
1 medium white onion,
  thickly sliced
2 Granny Smith apples,
  sliced
1/4 cup packed brown
  sugar
1/4 cup raisins
Sage, parsley, salt and
  pepper to taste
2/3 cup white wine

Yield: 6 servings

- Brown pork chops in skillet sprayed with nonstick cooking spray. Layer onion and apple slices over pork chops; sprinkle with brown sugar, raisins, sage, parsley, salt and pepper. Add wine.
- Simmer, covered, for 20 minutes or until pork chops, onion and apples are tender. Serve over rice or egg noodles.
- May substitute apple juice or cider for wine.

Beth R. Weaver

Marmalade Pork Chops

4 (3/4 to 1-inch thick)
  pork chops
1 tablespoon olive oil
1 cup wine
Rosemary and garlic
  powder to taste
1 cup lemon marmalade
  or other fruit marmalade

Yield: 4 servings

- Sauté pork chops in olive oil in skillet over medium-high heat for 2 to 3 minutes on each side or until light brown. Remove to baking dish.
- Add wine to skillet. Bring to a boil, stirring to deglaze skillet. Pour over pork chops; sprinkle with rosemary and garlic powder.
- Bake, covered with foil, at 350 degrees for 30 minutes. Spread marmalade over pork chops; baste with some of the pan juices. Bake, covered, for 20 minutes longer.

Bridget M. Weaver

Federal trials for treason of suspected Confederate sympathizers were held during the Civil War in the court room of the Custom House, now named West Virginia Independence Hall. The Atheneum stood where College Plaza is today. It was used as a Federal Civil War prison.

Pork Medallions

8 (4-ounce) pork
  medallions
1/4 cup flour
1/4 teaspoon pepper
1/4 cup (or less) olive oil
1 1/4 cups chicken broth
1/4 cup white wine
1 tablespoon white wine
  vinegar
1 teaspoon rosemary
2 medium scallions, sliced
2 tablespoons butter
4 ounces fresh
  mushrooms, sliced

Yield: 8 servings

- Coat pork with mixture of flour and pepper. Brown on both sides in olive oil in skillet; remove and drain pork.
- Add chicken broth, wine, vinegar, rosemary and scallions to skillet, stirring to deglaze. Cook over medium heat until slightly thickened, stirring constantly.
- Return pork to skillet. Cook until heated through. Remove pork to serving plate.
- Add butter and mushrooms to pan juices in skillet. Cook until mushrooms are tender. Spoon over pork.
- May serve over noodles or rice.

Beth R. Weaver

Creamy Pork Hash

This is an easy way to use leftovers.

1 medium onion, chopped
3 tablespoons butter
1 (10-ounce) can cream of
  mushroom soup
1/2 cup milk
1 teaspoon Worcestershire
  sauce
1/2 teaspoon Tabasco sauce
1 cup chopped cooked
  potatoes
2 cups chopped cooked
  pork roast
Salt and pepper to taste
Paprika to taste

Yield: 4 servings

- Sauté onion in butter in saucepan until tender. Stir in soup, milk, Worcestershire sauce and Tabasco sauce; mix well. Add potatoes, pork, salt and pepper.
- Simmer for 5 minutes or until heated through. Serve on toast points; sprinkle with paprika.
- May top with cooked peas.

Diana T. Ihlenfeld

Civil War soldiers, camped on Wheeling Island, were denied access to the Suspension Bridge at night. This action was taken to prevent soldiers from buying liquor in downtown Wheeling.

Indonesian Pork

4 medium onions, chopped
2 cloves of garlic, minced
3 tablespoons lemon juice
2 tablespoons brown sugar
1/4 cup soy sauce
4 teaspoons crushed
  coriander seeds
1 teaspoon each salt and
  pepper
1 1/2 pounds boned pork
  shoulder, trimmed, cut
  into 1-inch pieces

Yield: 6 servings

• Combine onions, garlic, lemon juice, brown
  sugar, soy sauce, coriander seeds, salt and
  pepper in glass bowl. Add pork.
• Marinate in refrigerator for 2 hours. Let
  stand at room temperature for 30 minutes.
• Drain pork; thread onto 6 skewers. Grill
  until pork is cooked through.

Jenny Miller

German Sauerkraut

1 to 1 1/2 pounds kielbasa
6 slices bacon
1/2 onion, chopped
1 small potato, grated
1 (16-ounce) can
  sauerkraut
1 cup chicken broth
1 cup apple sauce
1 tablespoon brown sugar
1 to 2 teaspoons caraway
  seeds

Yield: 4 servings

• Cook sausage using package directions.
  Cook bacon in skillet until brown. Remove
  and reserve bacon; drain most of the
  drippings.
• Add onion and potato to skillet. Cook until
  brown. Stir in sauerkraut, chicken broth,
  apple sauce, brown sugar and caraway seeds.
• Top with sausage. Simmer for 15 minutes or
  until heated through. Sprinkle with bacon.

Debbie Lucki

*It was the custom for boys to set off firecrackers on Christmas Day. The
description during the Civil War states that there was a
continuous popping, fizzing and blowing. Nervous people stuffed
cotton in their ears and took refuge in the remotest part of
their cellars or back buildings.*

Sausage Pilaf with Lemon

The lemon gives this a zesty twist.

8 ounces sweet Italian
  sausage
2 tablespoons olive oil
2 tablespoons margarine
1 clove of garlic, minced
1/2 cup chopped onion
1/2 medium green bell
  pepper, chopped
1/2 medium red bell
  pepper, chopped
1/2 cup chopped celery
1 tablespoon lemon juice
2 cups chicken broth
1 cup uncooked rice
1/2 cup grated Parmesan
  cheese
1/4 cup chopped green
  onions
1 tablespoon grated lemon
  rind

Yield: 4 servings

- Remove casings from sausage. Sauté in olive oil in 10-inch skillet until brown, stirring to break up sausage. Remove sausage and drain skillet, reserving 2 tablespoons drippings.
- Add margarine, garlic, onion, bell peppers and celery to reserved drippings in skillet. Sauté for 5 minutes.
- Add sausage, lemon juice and chicken broth. Bring to a boil. Stir in rice. Simmer for 20 minutes or until rice is tender. Stir in cheese, green onions and lemon rind.

Carol Tyler

Mom's Barbecue Sauce

This sauce has been perfected over the years.

3/4 cup catsup
1/2 cup water
2 1/2 teaspoons dry
  mustard
1 tablespoon
  Worcestershire sauce
2 tablespoons vinegar
1 tablespoon sugar
1 teaspoon celery seeds

Yield: 6 servings

- Combine catsup, water, dry mustard, Worcestershire sauce, vinegar, sugar and celery seeds in medium saucepan; mix well. Cook to desired consistency.
- Use to grill ham, beef, pork or chicken or in sloppy Joes.

Tammy Wright-Klemm

Coney Sauce

Kids love this.

8 ounces ground beef
1/4 cup water
1/4 cup chopped onion
1 clove of garlic, minced
1 (8-ounce) can tomato
  sauce
1/2 teaspoon chili powder
1/2 teaspoon MSG
1/2 teaspoon salt

Yield: 12 servings

- Brown ground beef in skillet, stirring until crumbly; drain. Add water, onion, garlic, tomato sauce, chili powder, MSG and salt; mix well.
- Simmer for 10 minutes. Serve over hot dogs in buns.

Patricia Phillips

Marinated Leg of Lamb

1 (5 to 6-pound) leg of
  lamb, boned, butterflied
2/3 cup lemon juice
1/2 cup packed brown
  sugar
1/4 cup Dijon mustard
1/4 cup soy sauce
1/4 cup olive oil
2 cloves of garlic, minced
1/2 inch sliced fresh
  gingerroot
1/2 teaspoon salt
1/4 teaspoon freshly
  ground pepper

Yield: 10 servings

- Place opened leg of lamb in 3-quart glass dish. Combine lemon juice, brown sugar, mustard, soy sauce, olive oil, garlic, ginger-root, salt and pepper in bowl; mix well. Add to lamb. Marinate in refrigerator for 2 hours to overnight, turning meat at least once.
- Drain, reserving marinade. Place fat side down on preheated grill 4 to 5 inches from coals. Grill, covered, for 15 minutes. Turn lamb. Grill for 10 to 20 minutes longer or until done to taste.
- Heat reserved marinade to a simmer in saucepan. Serve with lamb.
- If oven baking, place lamb in a large roasting pan, on a rack, fat side up. Broil for 20 minutes. Turn roast and broil for 20 minutes more. Test for desired doneness.

Joan Stamp

Wheeling was nicknamed the "Nail City." One quarter of the entire country's production was made in Wheeling. The iron cannon at LaBelle cut nail plant was made there during the Civil War. It is fired on momentous occasions.

Roast Chicken with Garlic and Potatoes

1 (3-pound) chicken
Salt and freshly ground
    pepper to taste
Unpeeled cloves of 1 large
    bulb garlic
4 bay leaves
2 teaspoons rosemary
1/4 cup olive oil
6 small red potatoes
1/2 large lemon

Yield: 4 servings

- Rinse chicken and pat dry inside and out; sprinkle cavity with salt and pepper. Cut 2 or 3 cloves of garlic into halves. Place in cavity with 2 bay leaves. Tie legs together; tuck wings under back. Rub inside and out with rosemary; sprinkle with salt and pepper.
- Heat oil in Dutch oven over high heat. Add remaining cloves of garlic. Sauté for 30 seconds. Add chicken, potatoes and remaining bay leaves. Sauté until chicken is brown on all sides.
- Squeeze lemon juice over chicken and potatoes. Bake at 375 degrees for 1 to 1 1/4 hours or until juices run clear, basting occasionally.
- Remove chicken, garlic and potatoes to platter; discard bay leaves. Spoon pan juices over carved chicken.

Linda Holmstrand

Apricot Chicken Divine

8 chicken breasts, skinned
1/2 cup unbleached flour
1 teaspoon salt
2 tablespoons olive oil
2 tablespoons melted
    margarine
1/3 to 1/2 cup apricot
    preserves
1 tablespoon Dijon
    mustard
1/2 cup nonfat yogurt
2 tablespoons slivered
    almonds, lightly toasted

Yield: 8 servings

- Rinse chicken and pat dry. Shake with mixture of flour and salt in plastic food storage bag, coating well.
- Spread mixture of olive oil and margarine in shallow baking pan. Arrange chicken in single layer in prepared pan. Bake at 375 degrees for 25 minutes.
- Combine preserves, mustard and yogurt in bowl; mix well. Spread over chicken. Bake for 30 minutes longer or until chicken is tender. Sprinkle with almonds. Serve over rice.

Shirley Trosch Milton

Buttermilk Chicken

12 chicken breasts
2 cups buttermilk
1 cup melted butter
1/2 teaspoon tarragon
3 tablespoons lemon juice
4 cups fresh bread crumbs
1/4 cup minced parsley
1/2 cup sesame seeds
3 tablespoons seasoned
   salt

Yield: 12 servings

- Rinse chicken and pat dry. Combine with buttermilk in shallow dish. Marinate in refrigerator overnight; drain.
- Combine butter, tarragon and lemon juice in bowl. Mix bread crumbs, parsley, sesame seeds and seasoned salt in bowl.
- Dip chicken into butter mixture; coat with crumb mixture. Arrange in baking dish. Bake at 350 degrees for 30 to 45 minutes or until cooked through.

Miriam King

Chicken Breasts with Bacon

6 chicken breast filets
8 ounces cream cheese
2 bunches green onions,
   chopped
9 slices bacon

Yield: 6 servings

- Rinse chicken and pat dry. Combine cream cheese and green onions in small bowl; mix well.
- Spoon cream cheese mixture on chicken; fold chicken over to enclose filling. Wrap each packet with 1 1/2 slices bacon; secure with wooden pick.
- Place on rack in broiler pan. Broil 6 to 8 inches from heat source for 30 minutes, turning once.

Miriam King

Wheeling had its first steam fire engine in 1864, but was the Vigilant Fire Company, located in North Wheeling, as vigilant as their name suggests? They were inside the firehouse when children alerted them to the fact that is was on fire. The building was destroyed.

Chicken Dijonaise

6 boneless chicken breasts
¾ cup mayonnaise
3 tablespoons Dijon
  mustard
2 tablespoons honey
4 teaspoons tarragon
  leaves

Yield: 6 servings

• Rinse chicken and pat dry. Arrange on rack in broiler pan. Spread top with mixture of mayonnaise, mustard and honey; sprinkle with half the tarragon.
• Broil for 6 minutes. Turn chicken and spread with remaining mustard mixture; sprinkle with remaining tarragon. Broil for 6 to 8 minutes longer or until cooked through.

Linda Gompers

Fantastic Chicken

10 chicken breasts,
  skinned
1 (8-ounce) jar apricot
  preserves
1 envelope onion soup mix
1 (10-ounce) bottle of
  Russian salad dressing

Yield: 10 servings

• Rinse chicken and pat dry. Place in shallow baking pan.
• Mix preserves, soup mix and salad dressing in bowl. Spread over chicken.
• Bake at 325 degrees for 1 hour.

Ella Jane Howard

*Wheeling Park was originally Hornbrook Park during the 1870s.
The beautifully landscaped estate was open to visitors who rode the open
air trolley from the city. They walked among the rare trees, shrubs,
and flowers while enjoying ice cream, lemonade, and other sweets.*

*Mozart Park overlooked South Wheeling. A $1,000,000 incline, longer than
two football fields, was able to carry 1,200 people an hour to the park. The
resort had a dancing pavilion for 5,000 people, an eight alley
bowling facility, a restaurant and a one-third mile long bicycle track.*

Grilled Chicken

1½ cups vegetable oil
¾ cup soy sauce
¼ cup Worcestershire
    sauce
¼ cup wine vinegar
2 cloves of garlic, crushed
⅓ cup fresh lemon juice
1½ teaspoons parsley
    flakes
2 tablespoons dry mustard
2¼ teaspoons salt
1 tablespoon pepper
8 chicken breasts

Yield: 8 servings

• Combine oil, soy sauce, Worcestershire
  sauce, vinegar, garlic, lemon juice, parsley
  flakes, dry mustard, salt and pepper in
  9x13-inch dish.
• Rinse chicken and pat dry. Add to marinade.
  Marinate in refrigerator overnight.
• Drain chicken and discard marinade. Grill
  chicken until tender.

Gay B. Kramer

Grilled Chicken Burgundy

⅓ cup Burgundy or other
    dry red wine
2½ tablespoons
    low-sodium soy sauce
1 tablespoon olive oil
1 clove of garlic, crushed
1½ teaspoons ground
    ginger
½ teaspoon dry mustard
4 chicken breast filets

Yield: 4 servings

• Combine wine, soy sauce, olive oil, garlic,
  ginger and dry mustard in bowl. Rinse
  chicken and pat dry. Add to marinade.
  Marinate, covered, in refrigerator for 4
  hours, turning once.
• Drain marinade into small saucepan. Bring
  to a boil; reduce heat. Simmer for 5 minutes.
• Place chicken on grill sprayed with
  nonstick cooking spray. Grill over
  medium-hot coals for 10 to 12 minutes or
  until chicken is tender, turning occasionally
  and basting frequently with marinade.

Holli Massey-Smith

*There was a daring attempt to rob the safe at the Custom House. The burglars
were after $1,250,000.00. Due to the construction of the vault, they were
able to break into the structure and to see and to feel the money, but they could
not get at it. They finally left the building by way of a second floor
window and a rope, leaving behind a lantern, crowbar, three
chisels, a handkerchief, and a bottle with about one drink left in it.*

Baked Mexican Chicken

4 chicken breast filets
1/3 cup melted butter
1 cup sour cream
1 (9-ounce) jar salsa
1/4 cup flour
Garlic salt and pepper to
   taste
1 cup crushed tortilla
   chips

Yield: 4 servings

- Rinse chicken and pat dry. Dip into melted butter; arrange in shallow baking dish.
- Combine sour cream, salsa, flour, garlic salt and pepper in small bowl; mix well. Spread over chicken; top with tortilla chips.
- Bake at 350 degrees for 1 to 1 1/2 hours or until tender. May add additional salsa if needed for desired consistency.

Kathy Tannenbaum

Mexican Chicken Divine Divan

This dish is great for a Mexican buffet.

4 whole chicken breasts
2 (10-ounce) cans cream
   of chicken soup
1 cup milk
1 (8-ounce) jar salsa
1/4 teaspoon each allspice,
   nutmeg and cinnamon
1 each green and red bell
   pepper, chopped
12 mushrooms, cut into
   quarters
2 tablespoons water
12 corn tortillas, cut into
   strips
1 pound Cheddar cheese,
   shredded

Yield: 8 servings

- Rinse chicken and pat dry; wrap in foil. Bake at 400 degrees for 1 hour or until tender. Tear chicken into bite-sized pieces, discarding skin and bones.
- Combine soup, milk, salsa, allspice, nutmeg and cinnamon in bowl. Mix bell peppers and mushrooms in bowl.
- Spread water in buttered shallow baking dish. Layer tortilla strips, chicken, green pepper mixture and salsa mixture 1/2 at a time in prepared baking dish. Sprinkle with cheese.
- Chill, covered, in refrigerator for 24 hours. Let stand at room temperature for 1 1/2 hours.
- Bake at 300 degrees for 1 1/2 hours.
- May use either green chili or tomato salsa in this recipe.

Jo Ellen Miller

Chicken Supreme

12 slices bread, crumbled
1/2 cup chopped celery
1/4 cup chopped onion
1 cup mayonnaise
3 or 4 chicken breasts, cooked, chopped
2 eggs
1/2 cup milk
1 (10-ounce) can cream of mushroom soup
1 (10-ounce) can golden mushroom soup

Yield: 8 servings

- Combine bread crumbs, celery, onion and mayonnaise in bowl; mix well. Layer half the bread crumb mixture, chicken and remaining bread crumb mixture in buttered 9x13-inch baking dish.
- Beat eggs with milk in bowl. Spread over layers in dish. Chill in refrigerator overnight.
- Mix soups in bowl. Spread over casserole.
- Bake at 350 degrees for 1 hour.

Mrs. Edgel E. Grose

Chicken Piccata

This is a great company dish.

2 whole chicken breasts, skinned, boned, cut into halves
Salt and pepper
1/4 cup flour
1/4 cup margarine
1/2 teaspoon minced garlic
2 cups sliced fresh mushrooms
1/4 cup dry white wine
2 tablespoons lemon juice
2 tablespoons chopped parsley

Yield: 4 servings

- Rinse chicken and pat dry. Pound 1/2 inch thick with meat mallet. Sprinkle with salt and pepper. Coat with flour.
- Brown in 3 tablespoons of the margarine in skillet over medium heat for 5 minutes on each side. Remove chicken from skillet and keep warm.
- Add remaining margarine, garlic and mushrooms to skillet. Sauté until mushrooms are tender. Add chicken, wine and lemon juice to skillet.
- Simmer for 8 to 10 minutes or until sauce is thickened to desired consistency. Sprinkle with parsley.

Caryn Buch

Chicken and Broccoli Casserole

2 cups chopped celery
1 cup chopped onion
1/4 cup chopped green bell
  pepper
8 ounces fresh
  mushrooms, sliced
1 pound fresh broccoli,
  chopped
1/2 cup margarine
1 1/2 pounds chicken,
  cooked, chopped
Garlic salt to taste
1 tablespoon salt
1 teaspoon pepper
16 ounces cream cheese,
  softened

Yield: 6 servings

• Sauté celery, onion, green pepper,
  mushrooms and broccoli in margarine in
  skillet until tender.
• Stir in chicken, garlic salt, salt and pepper.
  Add cream cheese. Cook over low heat until
  cream cheese is melted, stirring to mix well.
• Spoon into buttered baking dish. Bake at
  350 degrees for 1 hour or until golden
  brown.

Melissa Lucas Graham

Hot Chicken Salad

This is very good for showers and luncheons.

1 cup sliced or chopped
  almonds
2 tablespoons sugar
1 cup mayonnaise
2 teaspoons fresh lemon
  juice
1 teaspoon grated lemon
  rind
2 teaspoons grated or
  minced onion
1/2 teaspoon salt
2 1/2 cups chopped cooked
  chicken
1 cup chopped celery
1 cup crushed potato chips
1/2 cup shredded sharp
  Cheddar cheese

Yield: 8 servings

• Combine almonds with sugar in small
  skillet. Cook over medium heat until
  almonds are glazed and golden brown,
  stirring constantly.
• Combine mayonnaise, lemon juice, lemon
  rind, onion and salt in bowl. Add chicken,
  celery and almonds; mix lightly.
• Spoon into 1 1/2-quart baking dish; sprinkle
  with potato chips and cheese. Bake at 400
  degrees for 15 minutes or until heated
  through. Serve on bed of watercress if
  desired.
• May substitute shrimp, turkey or crab meat
  for chicken. May bake in individual baking
  dishes if preferred.

Cathy King

Swiss Chicken and Ham Bake

1/2 cup chopped onion
2 tablespoons butter
3 tablespoons flour
1/2 teaspoon salt
1/4 teaspoon pepper
1 (3-ounce) can sliced
  mushrooms
1 cup half and half
2 tablespoons dry sherry
2 cups chopped cooked
  chicken
1 cup chopped cooked ham
1 (5-ounce) can sliced
  water chestnuts, drained
1/2 cup shredded Swiss
  cheese
1 1/2 cups soft bread crumbs
3 tablespoons melted
  butter

Yield: 4 servings

- Sauté onion in 2 tablespoons butter in skillet until tender but not brown. Stir in flour, salt and pepper.
- Add undrained mushrooms, half and half and wine. Cook until thickened, stirring constantly. Stir in chicken, ham and water chestnuts.
- Spoon into 1 1/2-quart baking dish; sprinkle with cheese and mixture of bread crumbs and 3 tablespoons melted butter. Bake at 400 degrees for 25 minutes or until light brown.

Rosemary E. Miller

Roast Duck with Raspberry Sauce

1 (3 1/2 to 5-pound)
  domestic duck, dressed
Salt and pepper to taste
1 apple, cut into quarters
1 medium onion, cut into
  quarters
1/4 cup red raspberry jelly
1/4 cup water
1 1/2 tablespoons Dijon
  mustard
1 teaspoon lime juice
1/2 teaspoon salt
1/2 teaspoon pepper

Yield: 2 servings

- Remove and discard duck giblets and neck. Rinse duck inside and out; pat dry. Sprinkle cavity with salt and pepper. Stuff with apple and onion; secure cavity with wooden picks.
- Sprinkle duck with salt and pepper. Prick skin at 2-inch intervals. Place breast side up on rack in shallow roasting pan.
- Roast, uncovered, at 350 degrees for 2 1/2 to 3 hours or to 185 degrees on meat thermometer, basting occasionally; cover loosely with foil after 1 1/2 hours to prevent overbrowning.
- Combine remaining ingredients in small saucepan; mix well. Cook over low heat until heated through. Serve with duck.

Janie Altmeyer

Wild Ducks with Apple and Onion Gravy

This is a memorable meal.

2 wild ducks
Salt and pepper to taste
2 medium Granny Smith
  apples, chopped
1 medium onion, chopped
2 slices bacon
1 cup orange juice
2 tablespoons flour
1/4 cup orange juice

Yield: 2 servings

- Rinse ducks inside and out and pat dry. Sprinkle inside and out with salt and pepper. Stuff duck cavities with mixture of apples and onion. Place in roasting pan. Top each with 1 slice bacon; sprinkle remaining apple mixture around ducks.
- Roast at 325 degrees for 1 to 1½ hours or until tender, basting frequently with 1 cup orange juice and pan drippings.
- Remove ducks to serving plate. Pour pan juices with apples and onion into saucepan. Add apples and onion from cavities of ducks. Add mixture of flour and 1/4 cup orange juice gradually. Cook until thickened, stirring constantly.
- Carve ducks, discarding bacon. Serve with apple and onion gravy.

Laura Phillips Miller

The following is an excerpt from a letter by Anna Lyons Murphy, a student at Mount de Chantal Academy in the spring of 1882: "The 'Little Flappers of '82'—Jennie, Hilda, Bess—were in the habit of keeping tryst at the Grotto with several Wheeling swains. One lovely spring day Sister Jane Frances of the eagle eye spied the boys crossing the creek. End of the story!" From a letter by Bertha Loos Wolfe, Mount de Chantal student c. 1890: "Sister Mary Clare made the following announcement in the study hall: 'Young ladies, I do not want another invitation to graduation sent to Mr. Tom Miller. He already has twenty-four.'"

Turkey Breast Florentine

1 (3-pound) turkey breast
2 slices bacon, chopped
1/2 cup chopped onion
3 tablespoons flour
1/2 teaspoon crushed
   tarragon
Pepper to taste
1 1/2 cups milk
1 (10-ounce) package
   frozen chopped
   spinach, cooked,
   drained
1 (2-ounce) jar sliced
   mushrooms, drained
1 tablespoon melted butter
3 slices bacon
1/3 cup shredded
   American cheese

Yield: 6 servings

- Rinse turkey and pat dry. Place open on plastic wrap. Make 2 lengthwise slits to the right and left of the V; spread open. Top with plastic wrap. Pound to 1/2-inch thickness.
- Sauté chopped bacon in skillet just until crisp. Remove bacon, reserving drippings. Add onion to drippings. Sauté until onion is tender.
- Stir in flour, tarragon and pepper. Add milk. Cook until thickened, stirring frequently; remove from heat. Remove 1/2 cup of the sauce. Chill remaining sauce.
- Combine 1/2 cup reserved sauce with bacon, spinach and mushrooms in bowl. Place turkey skin side down on work surface. Top with spinach mixture. Roll turkey to enclose filling; secure with string.
- Place on rack in baking pan. Brush with butter; cover loosely with foil. Bake at 350 degrees for 1 1/2 hours.
- Remove string; top with bacon slices. Bake for 30 minutes longer or to 180 degrees on meat thermometer.
- Combine chilled sauce with cheese in small saucepan. Cook until sauce is heated through and cheese is melted. Serve with turkey roll.

Beth Ann Dague

The old woodcarver who designed the chapel altars at Mount de Chantal Academy had an assistant who turned out to be a convicted murderer from Germany. The nuns said his besetting fault was "love of gold."

Turkey Breast with Lemon Caper Sauce

This is wonderful for company.

1 cup parsley
5 large cloves of garlic
1¹/2 cups fresh lemon juice
1 cup vegetable oil
4 teaspoons crushed
  rosemary
1¹/2 teaspoons salt
Freshly ground pepper to
  taste
1 (5 to 6-pound) bone-in
  turkey breast
Salt to taste
6 tablespoons chilled
  unsalted butter
¹/4 cup drained capers

Yield: 12 servings

- Process parsley and garlic in food processor until chopped. Add lemon juice, oil, rosemary, 1¹/2 teaspoons salt and pepper, processing constantly for 3 minutes.
- Rinse turkey and pat dry. Combine with marinade in plastic food storage bag; mix to coat well. Marinate in refrigerator overnight.
- Let stand until room temperature. Drain turkey, reserving marinade. Place turkey in roasting pan. Sprinkle with salt and pepper to taste.
- Roast at 400 degrees for 30 minutes. Reserve ²/3 cup of the marinade. Roast turkey for 1 hour longer, basting with remaining marinade. Cool turkey while making caper sauce.
- Bring reserved ²/3 cup marinade to a boil in saucepan; remove from heat. Whisk in 2 tablespoons butter. Cook over low heat for several minutes, whisking in remaining butter 1 tablespoon at a time. Stir in capers.
- Cut turkey into thin slices. Serve over wild rice with caper sauce.

DeAnna Lee Taylor

Horned cattle were protected from annoyance by a city ordinance in 1876.
A newspaper reporter sarcastically suggested that the Council should pass
a law prohibiting people from the street during set hours for cattle-driving
through the city. The prior day a person had been gored by a steer.

Simple Saucy Fish Bake

1 pound white fish
1/2 teaspoon salt
1/8 teaspoon pepper
1 tablespoon butter
1 envelope Hollandaise
  sauce mix
1 (10-ounce) package
  frozen asparagus spears
Paprika to taste

Yield: 3 servings

- Arrange fish in ungreased baking dish, leaving space in center of dish. Sprinkle with salt and pepper; dot with butter. Bake at 475 degrees for 15 minutes.
- Prepare Hollandaise sauce using package directions. Cook asparagus using package directions. Place in center of baking dish. Spoon Hollandaise sauce over top; sprinkle with paprika.
- Bake for 5 minutes longer or until fish flakes easily. May sprinkle with 1 (3-ounce) can French-fried onions and bake for 2 minutes longer if desired. May substitute canned asparagus spears for frozen asparagus.

Cynthia Harvey

Sesame Roughy

4 orange roughy fillets
1 cup skim milk
1 cup flour
3 eggs whites, slightly
  beaten
1/2 cup sesame seeds
3 tablespoons butter
2 lemons, cut into halves

Yield: 4 servings

- Soak fish in skim milk for 30 minutes.
- Remove fish from milk and coat lightly with flour. Dip into egg whites and coat with sesame seeds.
- Fry in butter in skillet over medium heat until golden brown on both sides. Squeeze lemon juice over fish.

Vera Barton-Caro

Female waiters were prohibited from working at any place which sold intoxicating liquors in 1877. Liquor was not allowed to be sold by druggists unless there was a written prescription from a physician.

Salmon Nantua

6 salmon fillets
1 medium onion, chopped
8 medium mushrooms,
  sliced
1½ teaspoons butter
2 tablespoons flour
2 tablespoons melted
  butter
1 cup chicken stock
¼ cup whipping cream
1 cup mayonnaise
Tabasco sauce to taste
Salt and pepper to taste
8 ounces cooked shrimp
3 bay leaves
36 asparagus spears,
  steamed
12 cucumber slices

Yield: 6 servings

- Grill salmon until cooked through; keep warm.
- Sauté onion and mushrooms in 1½ teaspoons butter in large saucepan; remove with slotted spoon.
- Blend flour into 2 tablespoons melted butter in saucepan. Add chicken stock, cream, mayonnaise, Tabasco sauce, salt and pepper; mix well. Stir in shrimp, bay leaves and sautéed onion mixture. Cook over very low heat for 2 minutes or until thickened, stirring constantly; discard bay leaves.
- Arrange 6 asparagus spears on each of 6 serving plates. Top each with 1 salmon fillet. Spoon sauce over salmon; top with 2 slices cucumber. Serve immediately.

DeAnna Lee Taylor

Salmon Steaks

2 cups chicken broth
3 tablespoons chopped
  onion
3 tablespoons chopped
  parsley
1 bay leaf
¼ teaspoon salt
6 salmon steaks
¾ cup whipping cream
3 egg yolks
1 (10-ounce) package
  frozen chopped
  spinach, cooked
1 tablespoon lemon juice

Yield: 6 servings

- Combine chicken broth, onion, parsley, bay leaf and salt in skillet. Bring to a boil.
- Add salmon to skillet. Simmer, covered, over low heat for 8 to 10 minutes or until salmon flakes easily. Remove salmon to warm platter; discard bay leaf. Cook broth mixture until reduced to 1 cup.
- Combine cream and egg yolks in bowl; whisk until smooth. Add a small amount of the hot broth to egg yolk mixture; stir egg yolks into hot broth. Cook over low heat until thickened, stirring constantly.
- Stir in spinach and lemon juice. Cook until heated through. Serve over salmon.

Margaret M. Ewing

Baked Salmon Steaks

2 tablespoons lemon juice
¹/₄ cup packed brown
    sugar
4 salmon steaks
1 tablespoon melted
    margarine
4 thin slices lemon
8 teaspoons brown sugar

Yield: 4 servings

- Spread lemon juice in ungreased 9x13-inch baking dish; sprinkle with ¹/₄ cup brown sugar. Arrange salmon steaks in prepared dish; drizzle with margarine.
- Bake at 375 degrees for 15 minutes. Turn steaks; top each steak with 1 slice lemon; sprinkle with 2 teaspoons brown sugar.
- Bake for 15 to 20 minutes longer or until fish flakes easily. Serve with pan juices.

Hali Exley

Grilled Swordfish

2 tablespoons lemon juice
1¹/₂ tablespoons olive oil
2 cloves of garlic, finely
    chopped
2 tablespoons chopped
    fresh rosemary
¹/₄ teaspoon salt
¹/₈ teaspoon pepper
4 (1-inch) swordfish
    steaks

Yield: 4 servings

- Combine lemon juice, olive oil, garlic, rosemary, salt and pepper in shallow dish. Add swordfish steaks, coating well. Marinate in refrigerator for 1 hour or longer; drain.
- Grill over medium-hot coals for 7 minutes or until fish flakes easily, turning after 4 minutes.

Wendy F. Hinerman

"Wheeling Stogies," a type of cigar, were puffed in every state in the Union. Two hundred sixty-nine million, two hundred sixty-five thousand cigars were made in 1878; their cost was between three and five cents apiece. Wholesale family grocers, Flacous Brothers, manufactured over 20,000 pounds of mincemeat for Christmas in 1878.

Walleye in Wine

6 walleye fillets
Salt and pepper to taste
1 cup dry white wine
1/4 cup chopped green
  onions with tops
1/4 cup finely chopped
  green bell pepper
1/4 cup finely chopped
  celery
1 cup (or more) shredded
  Swiss cheese
1 cup Italian bread crumbs

Yield: 6 servings

• Rinse fillets in cold water and pat dry.
  Sprinkle both sides with salt and pepper.
  Arrange in greased 9x13-inch baking dish.
• Pour wine over fish; let stand for 10
  minutes. Sprinkle with green onions, green
  pepper and celery.
• Bake at 350 degrees for 25 to 35 minutes or
  until fish flakes easily, basting with wine
  once or twice. Sprinkle with cheese and
  bread crumbs. Broil until cheese melts.
  Serve immediately.

Judith McLaughlin

Crab Imperial

1 tablespoon flour
1 tablespoon melted butter
1/2 cup milk
1 teaspoon minced onion
2 slices bread, cubed
1 1/2 teaspoons
  Worcestershire sauce
1/2 cup mayonnaise
1 tablespoon lemon juice
1/2 teaspoon salt
Pepper to taste
2 tablespoons butter
1 pound lump crab meat
Paprika to taste

Yield: 4 servings

• Blend flour into 1 tablespoon melted butter
  in medium saucepan. Stir in milk gradually.
  Cook over medium heat until thickened,
  stirring constantly. Stir in onion, bread
  cubes and Worcestershire sauce. Cool to
  room temperature.
• Fold in mayonnaise, lemon juice, salt and
  pepper.
• Heat 2 tablespoons butter in large saucepan
  until light brown. Add crab meat; toss
  lightly. Fold in cooled sauce.
• Spoon into greased 1-quart baking dish;
  sprinkle with paprika. Bake at 450 degrees
  for 10 to 15 minutes or until bubbly and
  light brown. Garnish with lemon wedges
  and fresh parsley.

Adrienne P. Klouse

Lime and Ginger Scallop Sauté

¹/₃ cup walnut halves
1 pound sea scallops,
    patted dry
1 tablespoon olive oil
1 tablespoon unsalted
    butter
3 tablespoons fresh lime
    juice
Lime and Ginger Butter,
    chilled

Yield: 4 servings

• Spread walnuts on baking sheet. Toast at 350 degrees for 3 to 5 minutes or until golden brown.
• Sauté scallops in heated olive oil and butter in skillet over high heat for 2 minutes or until golden brown; drain skillet.
• Stir lime juice into skillet. Cook for 1 minute; reduce heat. Add Lime and Ginger Butter 1 tablespoon at a time. Cook just until sauce thickens. Stir in walnuts; garnish with parsley.

Lime and Ginger Butter

¹/₄ cup unsalted butter,
    softened
2 teaspoons grated lime
    zest
1 teaspoon ground ginger
¹/₂ teaspoon salt
Freshly ground pepper to
    taste

Yield: 4 servings

• Combine butter, lime zest, ginger, salt and pepper in bowl; mix well. Shape into 2¹/₂-inch roll. Chill, wrapped in plastic wrap, until firm.

Beth Ann Dague

Scallop Kabobs

12 slices bacon
16 sea scallops, cut into
    halves
2 (7-ounce) cans water
    chestnuts
¹/₂ cup soy sauce
¹/₄ cup light vegetable oil
2 tablespoons lemon juice
2 cloves of garlic
1 teaspoon minced
    gingerroot

Yield: 4 servings

• Soak bamboo skewers in water for 1 hour.
• Cut bacon into 2-inch pieces. Fry in skillet until light brown but not crisp; drain.
• Thread scallops, bacon and water chestnuts alternately onto skewers. Place in shallow glass dish.
• Process soy sauce, oil, lemon juice, garlic and ginger in blender.
• Pour over kabobs. Marinate, covered, in refrigerator for 3 to 4 hours, turning frequently.
• Grill over medium heat for 4 to 5 minutes on each side or until scallops are firm and white.

Cookbook Committee

Barbecued Shrimp

1/4 cup chopped onion
1 tablespoon brown sugar
1 tablespoon white vinegar
1/2 cup catsup
Hot sauce to taste
1 tablespoon dry mustard
1/4 teaspoon garlic powder
2 tablespoons fresh
   rosemary or 1
   tablespoon dried
   rosemary
24 jumbo shrimp
1 lemon, cut into wedges

Yield: 4 servings

- Heat nonstick skillet sprayed with nonstick cooking spray. Add onion. Sauté until tender; remove from heat. Stir in brown sugar, vinegar, catsup, hot sauce, dry mustard, garlic powder and rosemary. Let stand for 2 to 3 hours.
- Peel and devein shrimp. Combine with marinade in shallow dish, turning to coat well. Marinate, covered, in refrigerator for 1 hour.
- Soak four 8-inch wooden skewers in water for 30 minutes; drain. Drain shrimp. Thread skewers through both ends of shrimp.
- Grill for 3 to 4 minutes on each side or until shrimp turn pink. Squeeze juice from lemon wedges over shrimp.

Cynthia Harvey

Shrimp Seafood Casserole

All of the flavors in the casserole blend so that you would never know there is bread in it.

1 pound peeled cooked
   shrimp
2 cups shredded sharp
   Cheddar cheese
6 slices bread
2 tablespoons butter,
   softened
4 eggs
2 1/2 cups milk
1 teaspoon lemon juice
1/4 teaspoon dry mustard
1/2 teaspoon salt

Yield: 4 servings

- Layer shrimp and cheese in buttered soufflé dish. Spread bread with 2 tablespoons butter; arrange over cheese.
- Beat eggs slightly in bowl. Add milk, lemon juice, dry mustard and salt; mix well. Spoon over layers.
- Chill in refrigerator for 3 hours to overnight. Let stand until room temperature.
- Bake at 350 degrees for 50 to 60 minutes or until set and golden brown. May substitute crab meat for shrimp or lobster for half of the shrimp.

Sally B. Hart

Shrimp and Rice

3/4 cup chopped green
    onions
1/2 cup chopped celery
1 medium green or red
    bell pepper, chopped
1 tablespoon olive oil
1 (8-ounce) can tomato
    sauce
1/2 cup water
1 bay leaf
Parsley to taste
1 pound shrimp, cooked
6 cups cooked rice

Yield: 8 servings

- Sauté green onions, celery and bell pepper in olive oil in 2-quart saucepan for 5 minutes. Add tomato sauce, water, bay leaf and parsley.
- Simmer for 10 minutes. Stir in shrimp. Cook until heated through; discard bay leaf. Serve over rice or stir rice into sauce.
- May substitute white wine for water.

Barbara Whitehead

Enchiladas Pacifica

This recipe was developed after we tasted a dish like this in the San Francisco/Monterey Bay area.

1 medium onion, chopped
2 cloves of garlic, minced
1 (12-ounce) package
    imitation crab meat,
    chopped
2 (10-ounce) cans cream
    of celery soup
1 (4-ounce) can chopped
    green chilies
1 teaspoon ground cumin
2 cups shredded Cojack
    cheese
1 (10 count) package
    10-inch flour tortillas

Yield: 5 servings

- Sauté onion and garlic in skillet sprayed with nonstick cooking spray until tender but not brown. Add crab meat, 1 can soup, green chilies, cumin and half the cheese; mix well.
- Warm tortillas in oven or microwave until softened.
- Place 1/3 cup crab meat mixture on each tortilla. Fold sides of tortillas over to enclose filling completely. Place seam side down in 9x13-inch baking dish sprayed with nonstick cooking spray.
- Combine 1 can soup with enough water to make of pouring consistency in small bowl; mix well. Pour over enchiladas; sprinkle with remaining cheese.
- Bake at 350 degrees for 30 minutes or microwave on High for 20 minutes. Serve hot.

Judi Tarowsky

Frogmore Stew

This Low-Country seafood boil is usually served on paper plates around newspaper-covered picnic tables with plenty of ice-cold beer or soft drinks and iced tea.

1½ gallons water
3 tablespoons shrimp boil
3 tablespoons salt
2 pounds hot smoked link
  sausage or kielbasa, cut
  into 2-inch pieces
12 ears fresh corn, broken
  into 3 to 4-inch pieces
4 pounds unpeeled shrimp

Yield: 8 servings

- Bring water, shrimp boil and salt to a boil in large stockpot. Add sausage. Cook for 5 minutes.
- Add corn. Cook for 5 minutes; water need not return to a boil. Stir in shrimp. Cook for 3 minutes; water need not return to a boil. Drain and serve immediately.
- May use Old Bay Seasoning for shrimp boil.

Shirley Trosch Milton

Spicy Bayou Shrimp

3 tablespoons butter
½ medium onion,
  chopped
1 clove of garlic, minced
2 teaspoons creamy
  peanut butter
2 teaspoons lemon juice
1 teaspoon Old Bay
  Seasoning
3 tablespoons dry sherry
1½ pounds peeled
  medium shrimp
3 tablespoons butter
2 teaspoons chopped hot
  pepper
½ cup coarsely chopped
  peanuts
2 tablespoons parsley
  flakes
4 cups cooked rice

Yield: 4 servings

- Combine 3 tablespoons butter, onion, garlic, peanut butter and lemon juice in small bowl; mix well. Add Old Bay Seasoning and wine; mix well.
- Stir-fry shrimp in 3 tablespoons butter in wok for 2 to 3 minutes or until pink. Add peanut butter mixture and hot pepper. Cook for 2 minutes longer, stirring frequently. Add peanuts and 1 tablespoon parsley flakes. Cook for 1 minute longer.
- Toss remaining 1 tablespoon parsley flakes with hot rice in warm shallow serving dish. Spoon shrimp mixture over rice.

Kathy Tannenbaum

Sweet and Sour Shrimp

2 teaspoons soy sauce
2 tablespoons vegetable oil
2 tablespoons wine
vinegar
1¼ cups pineapple juice
2 tablespoons brown sugar
½ teaspoon ground ginger
Salt and black pepper to
taste
1 large green bell pepper,
cut into ½-inch strips
2 tablespoons cornstarch
6 tablespoons water
1½ pounds large Gulf
shrimp, peeled
¼ teaspoon cayenne
pepper
3 tablespoons vegetable oil

Yield: 6 servings

- Combine soy sauce, oil, vinegar, pineapple juice, brown sugar, ginger, salt and black pepper in saucepan. Bring to a boil; reduce heat. Add green pepper. Simmer, covered, for 3 minutes.
- Stir in mixture of cornstarch and water. Cook until thickened, stirring constantly. Remove from heat; keep warm.
- Cook shrimp with cayenne pepper in hot oil in large skillet for 5 minutes, stirring frequently. Arrange over bed of fried rice. Spoon warm sauce over top.

Beth Ann Dague

Seafood with Artichokes

½ cup flour
6 tablespoons melted
butter
2 cups milk
1 cup whipping cream
3 tablespoons catsup
1 tablespoon lemon juice
¼ cup sherry
½ teaspoon salt
¼ teaspoon cayenne
pepper
1 cup shredded sharp
Cheddar cheese
2 pounds peeled cooked
shrimp
1 pound lump crab meat
10 artichoke hearts,
chopped
1½ cups bread crumbs
3 tablespoons melted
butter

Yield: 8 servings

- Blend flour into 6 tablespoons melted butter in saucepan. Stir in milk, cream, catsup, lemon juice, wine, salt and cayenne pepper. Cook until thickened, stirring constantly. Stir in cheese until melted.
- Add shrimp, crab meat and artichokes; mix gently. Spoon into baking dish; top with mixture of bread crumbs and 3 tablespoons melted butter.
- Bake at 350 degrees for 30 minutes or until bubbly.

Miriam King

Seafood Bake

This recipe from Aunt Hen is great with a salad.

2 (7-ounce) cans crab meat
2 (7-ounce) cans shrimp
1 cup chopped green bell
  pepper
1/3 cup chopped onion
2 1/2 cups chopped celery
1 tablespoon
  Worcestershire sauce
2 cups mayonnaise
Paprika to taste
4 cups crushed potato
  chips

Yield: 6 servings

- Combine crab meat, shrimp, green pepper, onion, celery, Worcestershire sauce and mayonnaise in bowl; mix well.
- Spoon into 2 1/2 to 3-quart baking dish. Bake at 400 degrees for 15 minutes. Sprinkle with paprika. Bake for 5 minutes. Sprinkle with potato chips. Serve immediately.

Rosemary E. Miller

Paella Valenciana

2 cups (1/2-inch) chicken
  cubes
1 pound unpeeled shrimp
12 small clams in shells
8 fresh mussels in shells
6 small lobster tails in
  shells
1 small onion, chopped
1 green bell pepper, cut
  into strips
2 cloves of garlic, minced
2 tablespoons vegetable oil
2 (14-ounce) cans chicken
  broth
1 1/2 cups water
1/2 teaspoon salt
1 teaspoon pepper
1 teaspoon saffron
1 (2-pound) package rice
2 cups green peas
2 tablespoons chopped
  pimento

Yield: 12 servings

- Rinse chicken and pat dry. Rinse and clean shrimp, clams, mussels and lobster tails.
- Sauté onion, green pepper and garlic in oil in stock pot. Add chicken. Sauté until chicken is no longer pink.
- Add chicken broth, water, salt and pepper. Bring to a boil. Add saffron and rice; mix well. Place shrimp, clams, mussels and lobster tails over rice.
- Simmer, covered, for 30 to 45 minutes or until liquid is absorbed. Arrange rice and seafood on platter. Top with green peas and pimento.

Nini Zadrozny

Pasta

W H E E L I N G

Grand Opera House

At the location of 12th and Market streets, one can still see the angled corner entrance of the former Wheeling Opera Hall, later called the Grand Opera House, which had 1100 seats. An 1878 Wheeling newspaper article proclaimed the opening of the Opera Hall as "Announcement Extraordinary." The B & O Railroad ran trains from Barnesville, Benwood, and Bellaire for opening nights, February 5 and 6, 1878.

Many of the operas, concerts, and plays were performed in German. There were eleven German singing societies in the late nineteenth century in Wheeling, reflecting the heavy influence of the German immigrants.

Interestingly, Wheeling's love of the arts is still apparent, as Wheeling is the nation's smallest city to support a metropolitan class symphony orchestra.

photograph courtesy of Oglebay Institute Mansion Museum

Angel Hair Pasta with Fresh Vegetables

1 tablespoon salt
5 ounces uncooked angel
   hair pasta
2 tomatoes, chopped
2 to 4 cloves of garlic,
   minced
1 tablespoon vegetable oil
Basil to taste
2 green bell peppers,
   sliced
2 tomatoes, chopped
Grated Parmesan cheese
   to taste

Yield: 4 servings

- Add salt to enough water to cover pasta in saucepan. Bring to a boil. Add pasta. Cook using package directions; drain.
- Combine 2 tomatoes, garlic, oil, basil and green peppers in medium saucepan. Simmer over low heat until heated through. Stir in remaining 2 tomatoes.
- Combine with pasta in bowl; mix well. Sprinkle with cheese.

Melissa Cunningham-O'Rourke

Artichoke Pasta

1 (16-ounce) can
   artichoke hearts, cut
   into quarters
1 white onion, chopped
2 large cloves of garlic,
   minced
8 ounces mushrooms,
   sliced
1/2 teaspoon dried oregano
1/2 teaspoon fresh basil
1/4 cup skim milk or cream
3 tomatoes, chopped
1/2 cup (or more) white
   wine
4 ounces capellini pasta,
   cooked, drained

Yield: 2 servings

- Cook artichoke hearts, onion, garlic, mushrooms, oregano, basil and tomatoes in skim milk in large skillet. Stir in white wine.
- Simmer until vegetables are tender, adding additional wine if needed. Serve over pasta.

David Weaver

Thomas Edison made the first demonstration of an electric lamp in 1879. Three years later, Wheeling was the fifth city in the nation to have electric lights. Wheeling had a telephone line three years after Alexander Graham Bell invented the telephone.

Capellini Casserole

1 pound ground chuck
2 tablespoons butter
1 (24-ounce) can tomato
  sauce
Salt and pepper to taste
8 ounces cottage cheese
1/4 cup sour cream
8 ounces cream cheese,
  softened
1/3 cup chopped green
  onions
2 tablespoons minced
  green bell pepper
8 ounces capellini,
  cooked, drained
2 tablespoons melted
  butter

Yield: 8 servings

- Brown ground chuck in 2 tablespoons butter in skillet. Remove from heat; drain. Stir in tomato sauce, salt and pepper.
- Combine cottage cheese, sour cream, cream cheese, green onions and green pepper in bowl; mix well.
- Layer half the pasta, cottage cheese mixture and remaining pasta in 2-quart casserole sprayed with nonstick cooking spray.
- Pour melted butter over all. Top with meat sauce. Chill overnight.
- Bake at 350 degrees for 45 minutes.

Julie Squibb

Garlic Pasta with Mixed Vegetables

You may substitute any vegetables for the ones listed here. Added cooked chicken is tasty, too!

4 large cloves of garlic,
  minced
2 onions, chopped
2 teaspoons olive oil
1 (16-ounce) can tomatoes
1 each red, yellow and
  green bell pepper,
  chopped
8 ounces mushrooms,
  sliced
12 ounces angel hair
  pasta, cooked, drained
1/2 cup freshly grated
  Parmesan cheese
Salt and pepper to taste
All-purpose seasoning to
  taste

Yield: 6 servings

- Sauté garlic and onions in olive oil in skillet until translucent. Add tomatoes with juice. Cook until heated through, chopping vegetables with spatula.
- Combine peppers and mushrooms in steamer pan. Cook until tender.
- Combine garlic mixture with hot pasta in bowl. Stir in cheese. Sprinkle with seasonings. Add steamed vegetables; toss well. Serve with additional Parmesan cheese if desired.

Mary W. Renner

Fettucini al Pesto

3 cloves of garlic, minced
1/2 cup olive oil
1/2 cup butter
1 cup packed chopped
  fresh parsley
1 cup packed chopped
  fresh basil
1/2 cup half and half
1 teaspoon salt
1/2 teaspoon freshly
  ground pepper
1 cup freshly grated
  Parmesan cheese
2 pounds fettucini,
  cooked, drained

Yield: 8 servings

- Sauté garlic in olive oil and butter in saucepan until garlic is brown. Add parsley, basil, half and half, salt, pepper and Parmesan cheese; mix well.
- Simmer for 10 minutes, stirring frequently.
- Combine sauce and hot fettucini in bowl, tossing to coat. Serve immediately.

Cookbook Committee

Fettucini with Zucchini

8 ounces mushrooms,
  thinly sliced
1 clove of garlic, minced
1 pound zucchini, sliced
  into 2-inch strips
1/4 cup butter
1 cup whipping cream
1/2 cup butter
1 pound fettucini, cooked,
  drained
3/4 cup freshly grated
  Parmesan cheese
1/2 cup chopped fresh
  parsley

Yield: 4 servings

- Sauté mushrooms, garlic and zucchini in 1/4 cup butter in saucepan until tender. Add cream and 1/2 cup butter; mix well.
- Bring mixture to a boil; reduce heat. Simmer for 3 minutes, stirring occasionally.
- Add fettucini, tossing to coat. Stir in cheese and parsley. Serve with additional Parmesan cheese.

Cookbook Committee

For the first performance at Capitol Music Hall, the air was scented with perfume to enhance the ambiance.

Pasta

Shrimp and Pasta Primavera

1 (12-ounce) package
  fettucini
3 tablespoons butter
1/2 cup chopped onion
3 cloves of garlic, minced
1 1/2 pounds cooked shrimp
2 tablespoons butter
1 1/2 cups whipping cream
2/3 cup grated Parmesan
  cheese
1/4 teaspoon salt
1/8 teaspoon pepper
5 cups broccoli flowerets,
  cooked

Yield: 8 servings

• Cook fettucini using package directions;
  drain.
• Melt 3 tablespoons butter in skillet. Sauté
  onion and garlic in butter until tender. Add
  shrimp. Sauté for 2 minutes. Remove
  shrimp with slotted spoon.
• Add 2 tablespoons butter and cream to
  skillet. Heat until butter is melted. Stir in
  cheese, salt and pepper. Reheat slowly.
• Combine sauce and shrimp with fettucini in
  bowl; mix well. Serve over broccoli.

Margaret M. Ewing

Ham Lasagna

1/4 cup butter
1/3 cup flour
1/2 cup chopped onion
1/8 teaspoon garlic powder
1/8 teaspoon pepper
2 cups chicken broth
1 cup milk
1/2 cup grated Parmesan
  cheese
8 ounces mushrooms,
  sliced
8 ounces lasagna noodles,
  cooked, drained
1 bunch broccoli spears,
  steamed
16 slices cooked ham
8 ounces mozzarella
  cheese, shredded
1/2 cup grated Parmesan
  cheese

Yield: 8 servings

• Melt butter in saucepan. Add flour, onion,
  garlic powder and pepper; mix well. Stir in
  broth and milk. Cook until bubbly, stirring
  frequently. Stir in 1/2 cup Parmesan cheese
  and mushrooms.
• Layer half the noodles, broccoli, half the
  ham, mozzarella cheese, 1/3 of the milk
  mixture, remaining noodles, remaining ham
  and remaining milk mixture in 9x13-inch
  baking pan. Sprinkle with 1/2 cup Parmesan
  cheese.
• Bake at 350 degrees for 35 minutes. Let
  stand for several minutes before serving.

Sarah H. Koeniger

Lasagna

This is rich and delicious!

8 ounces uncooked
  lasagna noodles
1 tablespoon vegetable oil
1 pound pork sausage or
  ground beef
1/2 cup chopped onion
1 clove of garlic, minced
1 (16-ounce) can chopped
  tomatoes
1 (8-ounce) can tomato
  sauce
1 (6-ounce) can tomato
  paste
1 teaspoon dried basil,
  crushed
2 eggs
2 1/2 cups ricotta cheese
1/2 cup grated Parmesan
  cheese
2 tablespoons dried
  parsley flakes
1 teaspoon salt
1/2 teaspoon pepper
1 pound mozzarella
  cheese, thinly sliced
1/4 cup grated Parmesan
  cheese

Yield: 10 servings

- Cook noodles with oil using package directions; drain and rinse noodles.
- Brown sausage with onion and garlic in skillet; drain. Stir in tomatoes with juice, tomato sauce, tomato paste and basil. Simmer, covered, for 15 minutes, stirring frequently.
- Beat eggs in bowl. Add ricotta cheese, 1/2 cup Parmesan cheese, parsley, salt and pepper; mix well.
- Layer noodles, ricotta mixture, mozzarella cheese and meat sauce 1/2 at a time in 9x13-inch baking pan. Sprinkle with 1/4 cup Parmesan cheese.
- Bake at 375 degrees for 30 to 35 minutes or until heated through. Let stand for 10 minutes.

Gail E. Carl

In 1879, Wheeling was the largest manufacturing center in the United States in proportion to her population. There were six breweries with a number of German trained brewers. Four nail works and two glass houses owned and operated their own coal banks. Hobbs, Brockunier was the largest glass house in the nation by 1879.

Creole Mushroom Lasagna

This is a great vegetarian meal.

1 large onion, chopped
2 cloves of garlic, minced
1 tablespoon olive oil
1 (28-ounce) can whole
  tomatoes in purée
1½ cups dry white wine
1 bay leaf
1 teaspoon thyme
½ teaspoon salt
¼ teaspoon cayenne
  pepper
1 onion, chopped
8 ounces mushrooms,
  chopped
4 zucchini, chopped
1 tablespoon olive oil
¼ cup chopped parsley
1 teaspoon basil
½ teaspoon salt
¼ teaspoon freshly
  ground black pepper
1¼ cups shredded low-fat
  mozzarella cheese
15 ounces low-fat ricotta
  cheese
9 uncooked lasagna
  noodles
¼ cup shredded
  mozzarella cheese

Yield: 10 servings

- Sauté 1 onion and garlic in 1 tablespoon olive oil in skillet for 5 minutes or until tender. Add undrained tomatoes, wine, bay leaf, thyme, ½ teaspoon salt and cayenne pepper. Simmer for 30 minutes.
- Sauté 1 onion, mushrooms and zucchini in 1 tablespoon olive oil in skillet until tender-crisp. Add parsley, basil, ½ teaspoon salt and pepper. Cook for 2 minutes.
- Mix 1¼ cups mozzarella cheese and ricotta cheese in bowl.
- Layer zucchini mixture, uncooked noodles, cheese mixture and tomato mixture ⅓ at a time in 9x13-inch baking dish. Top with ¼ cup mozzarella cheese.
- Bake, tightly covered with foil, at 400 degrees for 40 to 45 minutes or until noodles are tender. Let stand for several minutes before serving.

Susan Wheeler

Coin glass was the most famous pattern of Central Glass Company. The glass pieces have imprints of U.S. silver coins on them which are usually dated 1892. The U.S. Government declared that the pattern was a form of counterfeiting. The glass molds were seized and production was stopped.

Spinach Lasagna

8 uncooked lasagna
  noodles
2 teaspoons minced garlic
1/2 cup melted butter
2 pounds ricotta cheese
2 eggs, beaten
1 tablespoon chopped
  parsley
Salt and pepper to taste
1 pound Monterey Jack
  cheese, shredded
1 cup grated Parmesan
  cheese
2 (10-ounce) packages
  frozen spinach, cooked,
  drained

Yield: 12 servings

- Cook noodles using package directions; drain.
- Sauté garlic in melted butter. Combine with ricotta cheese, eggs, parsley, salt and pepper in bowl; mix well.
- Layer noodles, ricotta mixture, Monterey Jack cheese, Parmesan cheese and spinach 1/2 at a time in buttered 9x13-inch baking pan.
- Bake at 350 degrees for 30 minutes.

Tammy Miller

Linguine with Artichokes

1 onion, finely chopped
1/4 cup olive oil
1 (14-ounce) can
  artichoke hearts
1/2 cup chicken broth
2 eggs
1/4 cup freshly grated
  Parmesan cheese
1 pound linguine, cooked
  al dente, drained
1/4 teaspoon salt
Freshly cracked pepper to
  taste
1/2 cup freshly grated
  Parmesan cheese

Yield: 6 servings

- Sauté onion in hot oil in skillet until transparent. Add artichoke hearts and broth. Cook over low heat for 5 minutes, stirring gently.
- Whisk eggs with 1/4 cup Parmesan cheese in bowl. Stir into skillet. Add noodles, stirring to toss. Sprinkle with salt and pepper. Stir in remaining 1/2 cup Parmesan cheese.
- Serve immediately.

Kathy Neidhardt

Wheeling Downs racetrack was confiscated from William "Big Bill" Lias
after he was convicted of income tax evasion.
The federal government later hired him to run the track.

Clams and Linguine

6 ounces uncooked
   linguine
2 tablespoons chopped
   garlic
Juice of 1/2 lemon
1 tablespoon olive oil
2 (6-ounce) cans minced
   clams
1/3 cup butter
1/2 teaspoon lemon juice
1 tablespoon parsley
Salt and pepper to taste

Yield: 3 servings

- Cook linguine using package directions; drain.
- Sauté garlic with fresh lemon juice in olive oil in skillet. Add undrained clams, butter, concentrated lemon juice and parsley; mix well.
- Bring to a boil. Simmer for 20 minutes. Sprinkle with salt and pepper. Serve over linguine.

Cindy Sloane Becker

Summer Linguine

This is a crowd pleaser. The fresh basil makes all the difference.

4 large tomatoes, chopped
1 pound Brie cheese,
   coarsely chopped
5 cloves of garlic, peeled,
   minced
1 cup chopped fresh basil
1 cup olive oil
1/2 teaspoon salt
1/2 teaspoon pepper
6 quarts water
1/8 teaspoon olive oil
1 tablespoon salt
1 1/2 pounds uncooked
   linguine
1/4 cup freshly grated
   Parmesan cheese
Freshly ground pepper to
   taste

Yield: 6 servings

- Combine tomatoes, Brie cheese, garlic, basil, 1 cup olive oil, 1/2 teaspoon salt and 1/2 teaspoon pepper in bowl; mix well. Let stand, covered, for 1 hour or longer.
- Bring water to a boil in saucepan. Stir in 1/8 teaspoon olive oil and 1 tablespoon salt. Add linguine. Cook for 8 to 10 minutes or until firm; drain.
- Toss hot linguine with tomato mixture in bowl. Brie will melt onto pasta. Sprinkle with Parmesan cheese and fresh pepper.

Caroline Bloch Jones

A company which began in Wheeling, Sterling Drug,
was the first to produce Bayer Aspirin.

Linguine with Shrimp

1 pound uncooked
 linguine
3 cloves of garlic, minced
1 tablespoon olive oil
10 Italian plum tomatoes,
 chopped
4 sun-dried tomatoes in
 oil, thinly sliced
3 cloves of garlic, minced
1 tablespoon olive oil
1 pound shrimp, peeled,
 deveined
8 ounces snow peas
1/2 to 3/4 cup white wine
1/4 cup chopped flat-leaf
 Italian parsley
1/4 cup grated Parmesan
 cheese

Yield: 8 servings

- Cook linguine *al dente* using package
 directions. Drain, reserving 1/2 cup cooking
 liquid.
- Sauté 3 cloves of garlic in 1 tablespoon olive
 oil in skillet. Add plum tomatoes. Cook for
 10 minutes. Stir in sun-dried tomatoes.
- Sauté 3 cloves of garlic in 1 tablespoon olive
 oil in skillet. Add shrimp. Sauté for 2
 minutes. Add pea pods. Sauté for 2 minutes.
 Add wine. Cook, covered, for 3 to 4
 minutes or until shrimp is done.
- Toss pasta with hot tomato sauce in bowl.
 Add shrimp mixture, reserved cooking
 liquid, parsley and Parmesan cheese; mix
 well. Serve with additional cheese.

Vilja K. Stein

Stuffed Shells

Tasty low-fat pasta

24 uncooked jumbo
 macaroni shells
1 (28-ounce) can tomatoes
1 (8-ounce) can tomatoes
1 teaspoon salt
1 teaspoon sugar
1/2 teaspoon coarsely
 ground pepper
1/8 teaspoon oregano
1/8 teaspoon basil
1 tablespoon canola oil
8 ounces ground turkey
15 ounces part skim milk
 ricotta cheese
1 (10-ounce) package
 frozen chopped
 spinach, thawed,
 drained

Yield: 8 servings

- Cook pasta using package directions; drain.
- Combine undrained tomatoes, salt, sugar,
 pepper, oregano and basil in 3-quart
 saucepan. Bring to a boil over medium-high
 heat, stirring frequently; reduce heat. Simmer,
 covered, over low heat for 20 minutes.
- Heat oil in 12-inch skillet. Add turkey.
 Cook for 10 minutes or until browned;
 remove from heat. Stir in ricotta cheese and
 spinach. Spoon into pasta shells.
- Spoon half the tomato mixture into 9x13-
 inch glass baking dish. Arrange shells in dish.
 Spoon remaining tomato mixture over top.
- Bake, covered with foil, at 375 degrees for
 40 minutes or until shells are heated
 through and sauce is hot and bubbly.

Donna Niess

Crêpes Manicotti

2 (15-ounce) cans tomato
  sauce with tomato
  pieces
2/3 cup dry red wine
2 cloves of garlic, minced
1 teaspoon basil
1 teaspoon oregano
1/2 teaspoon salt
1 teaspoon crushed red
  pepper
1/4 teaspoon black pepper
1 pound fresh
  mushrooms, sliced
1/4 cup butter
8 ounces mozzarella
  cheese, shredded
8 ounces ricotta cheese
1 egg
Chopped fresh mint to
  taste
Salt and pepper to taste
Crêpes
1/2 cup grated Parmesan
  cheese

Yield: 4 servings

- Combine tomato sauce, wine, garlic, basil, oregano, 1/2 teaspoon salt, red pepper and 1/4 teaspoon black pepper in small saucepan. Simmer for 20 to 25 minutes or until flavors are blended.
- Sauté mushrooms in butter in skillet over high heat for 4 to 5 minutes. Add to tomato mixture; set aside.
- Combine mozzarella cheese, ricotta cheese, egg and mint with salt and pepper to taste in bowl; mix well.
- Spread cheese filling on crêpes; roll to enclose filling. Arrange seam side down in buttered baking dish. Spoon tomato sauce mixture over top; sprinkle with Parmesan cheese.
- Bake at 350 degrees for 15 minutes or until bubbly.

Crêpes

2 eggs
3/4 cup water
3/4 cup flour
1/4 teaspoon salt

Yield: 4 servings

- Combine eggs, water, flour and salt in blender in order listed; process on High for 20 to 30 seconds. Scrape down sides of blender; process for several seconds longer.
- Spray crêpe pan with nonstick cooking spray. Heat over medium heat. Pour 2 to 3 tablespoons batter into heated pan, tilting to coat pan evenly; pour off excess batter.
- Bake until edges of crêpe are crisp. Turn crêpe. Bake until golden brown. Repeat process with remaining batter, spraying crêpe pan as needed. Stack crêpes between waxed paper until time to fill.

Jo Ellen Miller

Mostaccioli and Sauce

This is Dad Bizanovich's original recipe. We double the sauce recipe to have plenty of sauce.

4 cloves of garlic, chopped
1/4 cup olive oil
1 (29-ounce) can whole
   Italian tomatoes
10 large pitted black olives
1 (4-ounce) can
   mushroom stems and
   pieces, drained
Tabasco sauce to taste
1 tablespoon chopped
   parsley
1 tablespoon oregano,
   crushed
1 tablespoon sweet basil
Salt and pepper to taste
3 tablespoons brown sugar
1 pound uncooked
   mostaccioli
2 tablespoons olive oil

Yield: 8 servings

• Sauté garlic in 1/4 cup olive oil in skillet
  over medium-high heat until light golden
  brown. Add tomatoes, olives, mushrooms,
  Tabasco sauce, parsley, oregano, basil, salt
  and pepper; mix well.
• Simmer for several minutes. Add brown
  sugar gradually. Simmer for 30 minutes
  longer or until sauce is of desired
  consistency.
• Cook pasta using package directions for 12
  minutes or until *al dente*; drain. Toss with 2
  tablespoons olive oil in serving bowl. Add
  tomato sauce; toss to coat well.

Mary Lee Moore Bizanovich

Green Noodle Bolognese

1/2 cup finely chopped
   onion
1 small clove of garlic,
   minced
2 tablespoons olive oil
1 pound lean ground beef
1 cup sliced mushrooms
1 (16-ounce) can Italian
   plum tomatoes
2 tablespoons tomato
   paste
1/2 teaspoon sugar
1/2 teaspoon thyme
Salt and pepper to taste
8 ounces uncooked
   spinach noodles
3 tablespoons butter

Yield: 6 servings

• Sauté onion and garlic in heated olive oil in
  skillet until tender. Add ground beef. Cook
  until ground beef is brown and crumbly,
  stirring frequently. Add mushrooms. Cook
  for 3 minutes.
• Add tomatoes, tomato paste, sugar, thyme,
  salt and pepper. Simmer for 15 minutes,
  stirring frequently.
• Cook noodles using package directions;
  drain. Toss with butter in serving bowl. Add
  meat sauce; toss lightly. Serve immediately.

Beverly B. Fluty

Pasta with Pesto

1 pound very ripe
  tomatoes
1 cup fresh basil leaves,
  torn
3 cloves of garlic, minced
1 small red onion,
  chopped
Salt and pepper to taste
1 cup cold-pressed virgin
  olive oil
2 cups uncooked shaped
  pasta

Yield: 4 servings

- Place tomatoes in boiling water in saucepan
  for 1 minute. Plunge into cold water.
  Remove skin.
- Process basil, garlic and onion in blender or
  with mortar and pestle until smooth. Add
  tomatoes, salt and pepper; mix well. Mix in
  olive oil.
- Cook pasta using package directions; drain.
  Combine with pesto in serving bowl; toss to
  mix well.

Caroline Ihlenfeld

Pepperoni Rigatoni

1 clove of garlic, crushed
1 small yellow onion,
  chopped
2 tablespoons olive oil
2 or 3 ripe tomatoes,
  chopped
6 ounces pepperoni,
  thinly sliced
1/4 cup whipping cream
Salt and pepper to taste
8 ounces rigatoni, cooked
1/2 cup grated Parmesan
  cheese

Yield: 4 servings

- Sauté garlic and onion in olive oil in skillet
  until tender. Add tomatoes and pepperoni.
  Sauté for 3 minutes. Stir in cream, salt and
  pepper. Cook just until heated through.
- Toss with pasta in serving bowl. Top with
  cheese.
- May substitute Romano cheese for
  Parmesan cheese.

Jo Ellen Miller

From an 1885 tombstone:
*Stop strangers stop as you pass by
As you are now so once was I
As I am now so you will be
Prepare for death and follow me.*

Scallops with Vermicelli

1 pound bay scallops
2 tablespoons fresh lemon
  juice
2 tablespoons chopped
  parsley
1 medium onion, chopped
1 clove of garlic, minced
2 tablespoons olive oil
1 tablespoon butter
1¹/₂ cups chopped canned
  Italian tomatoes
¹/₂ tablespoon brown sugar
¹/₂ teaspoon basil, crushed
¹/₄ teaspoon oregano,
  crushed
¹/₄ teaspoon thyme leaves,
  crushed
1 tablespoon butter
2 tablespoons whipping
  cream
Nutmeg to taste
12 ounces vermicelli,
  cooked, drained

Yield: 4 servings

- Rinse scallops and pat dry. Combine with lemon juice and parsley in glass dish; mix well. Marinate, covered, for several minutes.
- Sauté onion and garlic in olive oil and 1 tablespoon butter in skillet over medium-high heat. Add undrained tomatoes, brown sugar, basil, oregano and thyme; mix well. Reduce heat to low. Simmer for 30 minutes, stirring occasionally.
- Drain scallops. Sauté in 1 tablespoon butter in skillet over medium heat for 2 minutes or until opaque. Add to tomato mixture; mix gently. Stir in cream and nutmeg.
- Combine with pasta in large bowl; toss to coat well. Serve immediately.

Julie Squibb

Vegetable Couscous

1¹/₄ cups chopped yellow
  bell pepper
²/₃ cup chopped red bell
  pepper
1¹/₄ cups chopped
  zucchini
5 tablespoons oil-free
  Italian salad dressing
6 tablespoons water
³/₄ cup uncooked couscous

Yield: 6 servings

- Spray large skillet with nonstick cooking spray. Heat over medium heat until hot. Add bell peppers and zucchini. Sauté until tender-crisp.
- Combine vegetables with 3 tablespoons salad dressing in bowl; toss to coat well. Set aside.
- Combine remaining 2 tablespoons salad dressing with water in small saucepan. Bring to a boil; remove from heat. Stir in couscous. Let stand, covered, for 5 minutes or until liquid is absorbed.
- Add couscous to vegetables; toss lightly.

Rosemary M. Front

Italian Meatballs and Spaghetti

1 pound lean ground
  chuck
1 cup very fine bread
  crumbs
1/2 cup milk
1/2 cup grated Parmesan
  cheese
2 eggs, beaten
1 tablespoon chopped
  parsley
1 teaspoon salt
1 teaspoon pepper
1 (32-ounce) jar spaghetti
  sauce
12 ounces spaghetti,
  cooked

Yield: 4 servings

- Combine ground chuck, bread crumbs, milk, cheese, eggs, parsley, salt and pepper in bowl; mix well. Shape into 1-inch balls.
- Place in baking pan. Bake at 350 degrees for 10 to 15 minutes or until cooked through, turning once or twice; drain.
- Combine with spaghetti sauce in saucepan. Cook until heated through. Serve over spaghetti.
- May also serve with a sweet and sour sauce or on wooden picks as appetizers.

Diana T. Ihlenfeld

Pasta with No-Cook Sauce

1 (6-ounce) jar marinated
  artichoke hearts
1 (7-ounce) jar roasted
  red peppers
1/4 cup chopped flat-leaf
  Italian parsley
2 tablespoons minced
  oil-pack sun-dried
  tomatoes
1 tablespoon chopped
  brine-cured black olives
3 tablespoons olive oil
1 tablespoon balsamic
  vinegar
1 tablespoon minced garlic
1/4 teaspoon freshly
  ground pepper
1 pound pasta, cooked

Yield: 6 servings

- Rinse, drain and chop artichoke hearts and roasted peppers. Combine with parsley, tomatoes, olives, olive oil, vinegar, garlic and pepper in bowl; mix well.
- Combine with hot pasta in serving bowl; toss to coat well.
- Serve immediately with grated Parmesan cheese.

Janie Altmeyer

Spicy Spaghetti

1 pound ground beef
1/4 cup chopped onion
1 (29-ounce) can tomato
  purée
1 (8-ounce) can tomato
  sauce
1 (6-ounce) can tomato
  paste
1 (4-ounce) can sliced
  mushrooms, drained
1/2 teaspoon each garlic
  salt, chili powder,
  oregano leaves, crushed
  red pepper, basil leaves,
  paprika, salt, pepper
  and parsley flakes
1 bay leaf
1 pound spaghetti, cooked

Yield: 6 servings

- Brown ground beef with onion in heavy
  saucepan, stirring until ground beef is
  crumbly; drain. Add tomato purée, tomato
  sauce, tomato paste, mushrooms, garlic salt,
  chili powder, oregano, red pepper, basil,
  paprika, salt, pepper, parsley flakes and bay
  leaf; mix well.
- Simmer, covered, for 2 hours, stirring
  occasionally. Discard bay leaf.
- Serve over hot cooked spaghetti.

Lisa Rae Sims

Spaghetti with Meatballs

4 cups tomato sauce
3 (6-ounce) cans tomato
  paste
1 envelope spaghetti
  seasoning mix
1/4 cup sugar
3 bay leaves
2 teaspoons basil
2 teaspoons oregano
1 teaspoon garlic powder
1 1/2 pounds ground beef
1 1/2 teaspoons chopped
  parsley
1 egg
1/2 cup Italian bread
  crumbs
1 teaspoon garlic powder
1 teaspoon salt
1 pound spaghetti, cooked

Yield: 8 servings

- Combine tomato sauce, tomato paste,
  spaghetti seasoning mix, sugar, bay leaves,
  basil, oregano and 1 teaspoon garlic powder
  in slow cooker; mix well. Cook on low heat
  for 6 to 8 hours.
- Combine ground beef, parsley, egg, bread
  crumbs, 1 teaspoon garlic powder and salt
  in bowl; mix well. Shape into 1-inch
  meatballs.
- Place meatballs in sauce in slow cooker.
  Cook for 1 1/2 hours or until meatballs are
  cooked through; discard bay leaves. Serve
  over spaghetti.

Caryn Buch

Williamsburg Pasta and Veal

This recipe may be prepared up to 2 days ahead or may be frozen and thawed in refrigerator overnight. Let stand at room temperature for 2 hours before baking.

12 ounces uncooked
   linguine
1 tablespoon vegetable oil
1 cup finely chopped
   onion
1/2 cup finely chopped
   carrot
1/2 cup finely chopped
   celery
1/4 cup butter
1 pound ground veal
1 (10-ounce) can chicken
   broth
1 teaspoon crushed
   tarragon
1 teaspoon salt
1/2 teaspoon pepper
1 pound mushrooms,
   thinly sliced
5 tablespoons butter
1/4 cup flour
1 1/2 cups milk
1 cup light cream
1 teaspoon salt
1/4 teaspoon pepper
1/4 teaspoon nutmeg
1 cup peas
1/2 cup grated Parmesan
   cheese

Yield: 6 servings

- Cook linguine *al dente* using package directions; drain. Stir in 1 tablespoon oil.
- Sauté onion, carrot and celery in 1/4 cup butter in skillet. Add veal. Cook until browned. Stir in broth, tarragon, 1 teaspoon salt and 1/2 teaspoon pepper. Simmer, partially covered, for 20 minutes.
- Sauté mushrooms in 2 tablespoons butter in large skillet. Remove mushrooms to bowl.
- Melt 3 tablespoons butter in same skillet. Add flour. Cook for 1 minute. Add milk and cream. Whisk until blended. Cook over medium heat until thickened; reduce heat. Add 1 teaspoon salt, 1/4 teaspoon pepper, nutmeg, peas and sautéed mushrooms. Simmer for 5 minutes.
- Spread 1/3 of the veal mixture in 7x11-inch baking dish. Layer linguine, remaining veal mixture and white sauce 1/2 at a time in prepared dish. Sprinkle with Parmesan cheese.
- Bake, covered, at 350 degrees for 45 minutes. Bake, uncovered, for 15 minutes longer.

Bridget M. Weaver

Wheeling celebrated the 400th anniversary of Columbus discovering America in 1892 with a four mile parade with 7,000 participants. There were two minor incidents: the decoration on a wagon burned when it struck an electric wire on Main Street; and the big globe on a float was ignited by a trolley wire on Market Street.

Vegetables & Side Dishes

SATURDAY OCT 5-01 10:30 A.M.

WHEELING

Wheeling Market House

The Wheeling Market House was located at the site of today's Market Plaza.

"Immense stores of meat and poultry; the tempting lumps of print butter; the piles of sacks containing Irish and sweet potatoes, etc.; the barrels and piles of apples, onions, turnips and vegetables generally; the big and little baskets of eggs, etc., etc." were items commonly available at the market in 1859. Slaves were also sold at this market house.

Although this market house has been razed, two market houses are still in operation in Centre Wheeling. The northern market house, built in 1853, in Centre Wheeling is the nation's oldest cast-iron market. Centre Market, as well as all of the historic buildings in the Wheeling business district, is listed on the National Register of Historic Places.

photograph courtesy of Ohio County Public Library

Asparagus Casserole

1 (10-ounce) can
  asparagus tips
1/3 cup butter
1/3 cup flour
1 teaspoon salt
1/4 teaspoon pepper
1 1/2 to 1 3/4 cups milk
1 pimento, chopped
4 hard-boiled eggs
1/2 cup shredded Cheddar
  cheese
1/2 cup fine bread crumbs
2 tablespoons melted
  butter

Yield: 6 servings

- Drain asparagus, reserving liquid. Reserve 6 tips for topping.
- Melt 1/3 cup butter in saucepan. Stir in flour, salt and pepper until blended.
- Combine reserved liquid with enough milk to measure 2 cups. Stir into flour mixture. Cook over low heat until of desired consistency, stirring constantly. Remove from heat. Stir in pimento and eggs.
- Layer asparagus and egg mixture 1/2 at a time in 8x12-inch baking dish. Sprinkle with cheese and bread crumbs; drizzle with 2 tablespoons melted butter. Top with reserved asparagus tips.
- Bake at 425 degrees for 20 minutes.

Shirley W. Weaver

Savory Beets

Best beets ever!

3 (16-ounce) cans sliced
  beets, drained
6 tablespoons vinegar
1/2 teaspoon ground cloves
1 teaspoon salt
1/2 cup sugar
1 small onion, sliced
1/4 cup butter

Yield: 8 servings

- Chop enough beets to measure 1 cup. Place remaining sliced beets in saucepan.
- Process 1 cup chopped beets, vinegar, cloves, salt, sugar, onion and butter in blender until puréed. Pour puréed mixture over sliced beets; mix well.
- Simmer for 20 minutes, stirring frequently.

Mary Frances Kase

*The West Virginia State Fair Association held its first
fair on the south end of Wheeling Island in 1881. The State Fair
in 1910 attracted 20,000 to 30,000 people each day.*

Carrots Au Gratin

2 cups chopped carrots
1/2 cup boiling water
Salt to taste
4 saltine crackers, crushed
1 teaspoon onion salt
1/4 cup chopped green bell
   pepper
1/8 teaspoon pepper
2 tablespoons melted
   butter
1/2 cup shredded sharp
   Cheddar cheese

Yield: 4 servings

- Combine carrots, boiling water and salt in saucepan. Cook for 10 minutes. Drain, reserving liquid.
- Combine crackers, onion salt, green pepper and pepper in bowl; mix well.
- Alternate layers of carrots and cracker mixture in greased 1-quart baking dish until all ingredients are used. Pour reserved liquid over layers. Drizzle with butter; sprinkle with cheese.
- Bake at 425 degrees for 15 to 20 minutes or until cheese melts.

Rebecca Sinclair

Cauliflower Soufflé

Excellent vegetable side dish

1 large head cauliflower
1/3 cup butter
2 tablespoons flour
1 cup milk
3 egg yolks
3 egg whites, stiffly beaten
1/4 cup grated Parmesan
   cheese
Salt and pepper to taste

Yield: 6 servings

- Steam cauliflower in steamer until tender. Separate into flowerets, discarding stem.
- Arrange flowerets in 2-quart soufflé dish sprayed with nonstick cooking spray.
- Melt butter in saucepan. Stir in flour and milk gradually. Cook until thickened, stirring constantly. Remove from heat.
- Stir a small amount of hot mixture into egg yolks; stir egg yolks into hot mixture. Cool.
- Fold egg whites and cheese into egg mixture. Season with salt and pepper. Pour over cauliflowerets.
- Bake at 350 degrees for 30 to 45 minutes or until soufflé tests done. May cover loosely with foil to prevent excess browning.

Susie Pere

Corn Pudding

Traditional frontier flavor

2 eggs
1/2 cup sugar
3 tablespoons flour
Salt to taste
1/2 cup milk
2 (17-ounce) cans whole
   kernel corn, drained
1/4 cup melted margarine

Yield: 6 to 8 servings

- Beat eggs and sugar in mixer bowl until blended. Stir in flour, salt, milk, corn and melted margarine. Spoon into greased 1 1/2-quart baking dish.
- Bake at 350 degrees for 50 to 60 minutes or until set.
- May use 1/2 cup egg substitute instead of eggs.

Melissa Lucas Graham

Sautéed Corn and Broccoli

1/2 cup butter
1 (10-ounce) package
   frozen broccoli, thawed,
   coarsely chopped
1 (10-ounce) package
   frozen whole kernel
   corn, thawed, drained
1 (4-ounce) can sliced
   mushrooms, drained
3 tablespoons sliced
   almonds
Salt and pepper to taste

Yield: 5 servings

- Melt butter in large skillet. Stir in broccoli, corn, mushrooms, almonds, salt and pepper.
- Sauté for 10 to 15 minutes or until done to taste, stirring frequently.

Ann Bopp

In the Wheeling of 1896, one of the first signs of spring was the organ grinder with his monkey. There were German bands that played on the street and passed the hat. There were also performing bears, gypsy fortune tellers, and fakirs selling trinkets.

Stuffed Eggplant

You do not have to like eggplant to love this dish!

2 (1¹/₄-pound) eggplant
Salt to taste
¹/₄ cup finely chopped
  onion
³/₄ cup sliced celery
¹/₄ cup margarine
2 (10-ounce) cans cream
  of mushroom soup
2 tablespoons parsley
  flakes
1 teaspoon seasoned salt
1 teaspoon oregano
2 medium tomatoes,
  peeled, chopped
3 cups corn Chex, crushed
¹/₂ cup grated Parmesan
  cheese
¹/₄ cup shredded brick
  cheese

Yield: 10 servings

- Cut off a lengthwise slice ¹/₃ way down each eggplant. Scoop out pulp carefully, leaving ¹/₄-inch shell. Combine shells and salt to taste with enough water to cover in large bowl. Set aside.
- Combine eggplant pulp and salt to taste with enough water to cover in saucepan. Simmer for 15 minutes or until tender, stirring occasionally; drain.
- Sauté onion and celery in margarine in skillet for 5 to 10 minutes or until vegetables are tender. Stir in soup, parsley flakes, seasoned salt and oregano. Add tomatoes, corn Chex, Parmesan cheese and eggplant; mix well.
- Drain shells; fill with eggplant mixture. Sprinkle with brick cheese. Place on baking sheet.
- Bake at 350 degrees for 20 to 25 minutes or until cheese is melted.

Mary Frances Kase

Marinated Green Beans

4 to 6 (16-ounce) cans
  whole green beans
1 cup cider vinegar
1 tablespoon sugar
1 tablespoon dillweed
1 tablespoon MSG
1 teaspoon salt
Coarsely ground pepper
  to taste
1 tablespoon garlic salt
1 cup vegetable oil

Yield: 18 servings

- Place green beans in colander. Pour boiling water over beans; drain.
- Combine beans with mixture of vinegar, sugar, dillweed, MSG, salt, pepper, garlic salt and oil in bowl; mix well.
- Marinate, covered, in refrigerator; drain.
- May substitute 3 pounds raw or blanched broccoli or cooked Brussels sprouts for green beans.

Ella Jane Howard

Tangy Green Beans

Salt to taste
1 pound fresh green
  beans, trimmed
1 lemon
4 cloves of garlic, minced
6 tablespoons olive oil
1/2 teaspoon coarsely
  ground pepper
1/4 cup grated Parmesan
  cheese

Yield: 4 servings

- Bring 2 inches lightly salted water to a boil in 2-quart saucepan. Stir in green beans.
- Cook, covered, for 8 minutes or until tender-crisp; drain
- Remove rind from lemon; cut into 1 1/2-inch strips. Squeeze juice from lemon. Set aside.
- Sauté garlic in olive oil in saucepan for 1 to 2 minutes or until light brown. Add beans, tossing to coat. Stir in lemon strips, lemon juice and pepper; mix well.
- Spoon into heated serving dish; sprinkle with cheese. Serve immediately.

Vera Barton-Caro

Roasted Mushrooms and Peppers

2 pounds fresh mushrooms
1 red bell pepper, cut into
  strips
1 green bell pepper, cut
  into strips
1/3 cup vegetable oil
2 cloves of garlic, crushed
Salt to taste

Yield: 6 servings

- Arrange mushrooms, red pepper and green pepper in 9x13-inch baking dish.
- Pour mixture of oil and garlic over vegetables, tossing to coat.
- Bake, covered with foil, at 300 degrees for 30 minutes, stirring once. Season with salt.
- Serve immediately.

Carol Tyler

Onion Casserole

4 to 6 large onions,
  thickly sliced
1/2 cup butter
1 (10-ounce) can cream of
  mushroom soup
1 tablespoon soy sauce
8 ounces Swiss cheese,
  chopped

Yield: 4 servings

- Sauté onions in butter in skillet until tender.
- Stir in soup, soy sauce and cheese. Spoon into baking dish.
- Bake at 350 degrees for 30 minutes or until bubbly.

Caroline Bloch Jones

Twice-Baked Bleu Cheese Potatoes

An adaptation of my grandmother's recipe. Men love this!

6 baking potatoes
Vegetable oil to taste
1/4 cup butter
Milk to taste
1 cup sour cream
1 teaspoon salt
3 tablespoons crumbled
  bleu cheese
2 tablespoons minced
  chives

Yield: 6 servings

- Rub potato skins with oil; pierce with fork. Place on baking sheet.
- Bake at 450 degrees for 45 minutes or until tender.
- Slice top from potatoes. Scoop out pulp carefully, leaving shells.
- Beat potato pulp, butter, milk, sour cream and salt in mixer bowl until light and fluffy. Stir in bleu cheese and chives.
- Fill reserved shells with potato mixture. Place on baking sheet.
- Bake for 8 to 10 minutes or until heated through

Deborah D. Wright

Perogie Casserole

Eastern European comfort food

10 to 12 medium
  potatoes, cooked
8 ounces Cheddar cheese,
  shredded
Salt and pepper to taste
Milk to taste
2 medium-to-large onions,
  chopped
1 cup margarine
9 to 12 lasagna noodles,
  cooked, drained
4 ounces Cheddar cheese,
  shredded
Parsley flakes to taste

Yield: 10 servings

- Mash potatoes with 8 ounces cheese, salt and pepper in bowl. Add just enough milk to make of thick spreading consistency.
- Sauté onions in margarine in skillet.
- Layer noodles, 1/2 of the potato mixture and onion mixture in 9x13-inch baking dish sprayed with nonstick cooking spray. Spread remaining potato mixture over onions; sprinkle with 4 ounces cheese and parsley.
- Bake, covered, at 350 degrees for 30 to 35 minutes or until bubbly.

Nini Zadrozny

Potpourri Potatoes

The tantalizing aroma accounts for the name.

2 pounds unpeeled small
  new potatoes, cut into
  bite-sized pieces
2 tablespoons olive oil
4 to 6 cloves of garlic,
  thinly sliced
1/2 teaspoon marjoram
1/2 teaspoon thyme
1/2 teaspoon rosemary
1/4 teaspoon salt
1/2 teaspoon freshly
  ground pepper
Lemon juice to taste
1 tablespoon chopped
  fresh parsley

Yield: 6 servings

- Combine potatoes, olive oil, garlic,
  marjoram, thyme, rosemary, salt and pepper
  in bowl; mix well. Place in baking pan.
- Bake at 350 degrees for 1 hour or until
  potatoes are tender and golden brown,
  stirring 2 to 3 times.
- Drizzle with lemon juice; sprinkle with
  parsley.

Jo Ellen Miller

Potato-Spinach Casserole

This may be served as an entrée or as a side dish with ham.

1 (10-ounce) package
  frozen chopped
  spinach, thawed
6 to 8 large potatoes,
  peeled, cut into
  quarters, cooked
3/4 cup sour cream
1 teaspoon salt
1 teaspoon pepper
1 teaspoon sugar
1/4 cup margarine,
  softened
2 to 3 green onions,
  chopped
1/4 teaspoon dillweed
1 cup shredded Cheddar
  cheese

Yield: 6 servings

- Squeeze moisture from spinach.
- Mash potatoes in bowl. Beat in sour cream,
  salt, pepper, sugar and margarine until
  smooth. Stir in green onions and dillweed.
- Fold in spinach.
- Spoon into baking dish; sprinkle with
  cheese. Chill, covered, overnight.
- Bake at 400 degrees for 20 minutes.

Jo Ellen Miller

Swedish Potatoes

Feeds a crowd!

6 to 8 potatoes, cooked,
  peeled, chopped
Salt and pepper to taste
1 cup chopped green
  onions
1 cup chopped green bell
  pepper
1 cup chopped celery
1 (2-ounce) jar pimento,
  drained, chopped
1 pound Velveeta cheese,
  chopped
1 cup whipping cream
8 ounces bacon,
  crisp-fried, crumbled

Yield: 10 servings

- Layer potatoes, salt, pepper, green onions, green pepper, celery, pimento and Velveeta cheese in greased 9x13-inch baking dish.
- Pour whipping cream over layers; sprinkle with bacon.
- Bake at 350 degrees for 45 minutes.

Rebecca Sinclair

Zucchini Potatoes

Beautiful twice-baked variation

4 medium baking potatoes
1/2 cup light or heavy
  cream
2 small zucchini with
  skins, grated
1 clove of garlic, minced
1/2 cup butter
Salt and pepper to taste
Paprika to taste

Yield: 6 servings

- Bake potatoes until tender. Cut into halves lengthwise. Scoop pulp into bowl, reserving shells. Add cream to pulp. Mash mixture until smooth.
- Sauté zucchini and garlic in butter in skillet until tender. Stir into potato mixture; season with salt and pepper. Spoon into reserved potato shells; place in baking dish. Sprinkle with paprika.
- Bake at 350 degrees for 10 minutes.

Diana T. Ihlenfeld

*Many of the stained glass windows at
St. Matthew's Church are Tiffany.*

Spinach Casserole

2 (10-ounce) packages
  frozen spinach, cooked,
  drained
8 ounces cream cheese,
  softened
1/4 cup melted margarine
Salt and pepper to taste
1 cup herb-seasoned
  stuffing mix
1/4 cup melted margarine

Yield: 6 servings

- Combine spinach, cream cheese, 1/4 cup melted margarine, salt and pepper in bowl; mix well. Spoon into loaf pan sprayed with nonstick cooking spray. Top with stuffing mix; drizzle with 1/4 cup melted margarine.
- Bake at 300 degrees for 20 to 30 minutes or until brown.

Linda Peterson

Acorn Squash

2 (1 1/4-pound) acorn
  squash
1 cup chopped unpeeled
  apple
1/4 to 1/2 cup orange juice
1/4 cup packed brown
  sugar
1/4 cup melted butter
1/4 cup chopped salted
  pecans, toasted

Yield: 4 servings

- Cut squash into halves; discard seeds. Trim bottoms. Place cut side up in shallow baking dish. Add 1/2 inch boiling water.
- Combine apple and orange juice to cover in bowl; mix well. Stir in brown sugar and butter. Spoon into squash shells.
- Bake, covered, at 350 degrees for 1 hour or until squash is tender. Top with pecans.

Janie Altmeyer

Grilled Squash

A tangy variation

2 medium zucchini
1/4 cup olive oil
1/4 cup balsamic vinegar
Salt and pepper to taste

Yield: 4 servings

- Cut zucchini into halves lengthwise.
- Pour mixture of olive oil, balsamic vinegar, salt and pepper into shallow glass dish. Place zucchini cut side down in olive oil mixture.
- Marinate at room temperature for 1 hour, turning once.
- Grill over hot coals until tender, turning once; baste frequently.

Janie Altmeyer

Squash Sauté

1/4 cup chopped onion
2 cloves of garlic, chopped
1 tablespoon vegetable oil
2 cups chopped tomatoes
3/4 teaspoon basil
1/4 teaspoon tarragon
1/2 teaspoon salt
1/8 teaspoon pepper
2 tablespoons tomato
  paste
3 cups sliced zucchini
3 cups sliced yellow
  squash

Yield: 4 servings

- Sauté onion and garlic in oil in saucepan for 3 minutes or until tender. Stir in tomatoes, basil, tarragon, salt and pepper.
- Bring mixture to a boil, stirring frequently; reduce heat. Stir in tomato paste.
- Simmer for 15 minutes, stirring occasionally. Add zucchini and yellow squash; mix well.
- Simmer for 15 minutes, stirring occasionally. Serve with freshly grated Parmesan cheese.

Samantha Hensel Buch

Scalloped Tomatoes and Artichoke Hearts

Elegant side dish

2 (28-ounce) cans whole
  tomatoes, drained
1 (14-ounce) can
  artichoke hearts,
  rinsed, cut into quarters
1/2 cup chopped onion
2 tablespoons chopped
  green onions
1/2 cup margarine
1/2 teaspoon basil
2 tablespoons sugar
Salt and pepper to taste

Yield: 10 servings

- Arrange tomatoes and artichokes in greased baking dish.
- Sauté onion and green onions in margarine in skillet. Stir in basil, sugar, salt and pepper. Spoon over tomatoes and artichokes.
- Bake at 325 degrees until heated through.

Sara R. Meek

Stifel & Sons was one of the nation's largest calico printing establishments. In the early 1900s the calico produced by Stifel was printed with their distinctive "boot" trademark.

Baked Cheesy Tomatoes

5 medium tomatoes, cut
 into halves
Italian salad dressing to
 taste
3/4 teaspoon salt
1 cup soft bread crumbs
1 cup shredded
 mozzarella cheese
1/4 cup melted butter
1 teaspoon whole basil
1/2 teaspoon red pepper

Yield: 10 servings

• Brush cut side of tomatoes with salad
  dressing; sprinkle with salt. Arrange in
  9x13-inch baking dish.
• Combine bread crumbs, cheese, melted
  butter, basil and red pepper in bowl; mix
  well. Spoon over cut surfaces of tomatoes.
• Bake at 350 degrees for 12 to 15 minutes or
  until cheese is melted and tomatoes are
  heated through.

Lisa Rae Sims

Cherry Tomatoes with Garlic Butter

1 tablespoon unsalted
 butter
1 pint cherry tomatoes,
 stems removed
1/2 teaspoon salt
Ground pepper to taste
2 tablespoons chopped
 fresh basil
2 tablespoons chopped
 fresh parsley
2 tablespoons thinly
 sliced green onions
2 large cloves of garlic,
 minced
1 tablespoon unsalted
 butter

Yield: 4 servings

• Melt 1 tablespoon butter in skillet over
  medium heat. Stir in cherry tomatoes, salt
  and pepper. Sauté for 3 minutes, swirling
  pan occasionally; skins will begin to split.
  Stir in basil, parsley, green onions and garlic.
• Cook for 2 minutes, stirring occasionally;
  reduce heat.
• Stir in 1 tablespoon butter, swirling pan to
  coat tomatoes. Serve immediately.

Carol Tyler

*Stifel calico was exported to Latin America, India, the Philippine
Islands, Canada and Africa. A story is told that Africans
frequently wore their calico clothes inside-out to display the boot
trademark—an early designer label!*

Zucchini and Tomatoes Au Gratin

2 tablespoons chopped
  onion
1 tablespoon butter
4 ounces zucchini, cut
  into 1/2-inch pieces
1/2 cup cooked tomatoes
1/4 teaspoon salt
Pepper to taste
1/4 cup shredded Cheddar
  cheese

Yield: 2 servings

- Sauté onion in butter in saucepan for 2 to 3 minutes or until tender. Stir in zucchini.
- Cook over low heat for 5 minutes, stirring frequently. Stir in tomatoes, salt and pepper.
- Cook, covered, for 5 minutes, stirring occasionally. Spoon into greased baking dish; sprinkle with cheese.
- Bake at 375 degrees for 15 minutes or until cheese melts.

Ella Jane Howard

Sweet Potato Casserole

Southern favorite!

3 cups mashed cooked
  sweet potatoes
1 cup sugar
2 eggs
1 teaspoon vanilla extract
1/3 cup milk
1/2 cup butter, softened
1 cup packed brown sugar
1/3 cup flour
1/3 cup butter, softened
1 cup finely chopped
  pecans

Yield: 8 servings

- Combine sweet potatoes, sugar, eggs, vanilla, milk and 1/2 cup butter in mixer bowl. Beat until smooth. Spoon into 9x13-inch baking pan.
- Sprinkle with mixture of brown sugar, flour, 1/3 cup butter and pecans.
- Bake at 350 degrees for 30 minutes.

Kathy Mitchell

*In the late 1800s, men joined volunteer fire brigades
for camaraderie, as well as to fight fires.*

Louisiana Yams

Good with ham or turkey

2 (16-ounce) cans yams,
   drained
2 eggs
1/4 cup melted butter
1/4 cup rum
1/2 cup packed brown
   sugar
1/4 teaspoon cinnamon
3/4 teaspoon salt
1/2 cup chopped pecans
2/3 cup shredded coconut
1 tablespoon melted butter
1 (11-ounce) can
   mandarin oranges,
   drained
1 tablespoon melted butter

Yield: 8 servings

- Mash yams in large mixer bowl. Add eggs, 1/4 cup melted butter, rum, brown sugar, cinnamon and salt. Beat until light and fluffy. Stir in pecans. Spoon into greased 1-quart baking dish.
- Bake at 325 degrees for 35 minutes.
- Toss coconut with 1 tablespoon melted butter in bowl. Sprinkle around edge of baking dish; arrange mandarin oranges next to coconut. Drizzle with 1 tablespoon melted butter.
- Bake for 10 to 15 minutes or until coconut is light brown.

Ann Vieweg

Baked Fruit Casserole

Serve for breakfast, brunch, as a side dish or as an appetizer.

1 (20-ounce) can sliced
   peaches, drained
1 (20-ounce) can sliced
   pears, drained
1 (20-ounce) can
   pineapple chunks,
   drained
3/4 cup packed brown
   sugar
1/3 cup melted margarine
1 teaspoon ginger

Yield: 8 servings

- Cut peaches, pears and pineapple into bite-sized pieces. Arrange in 3-quart baking dish.
- Sprinkle fruit with mixture of brown sugar, margarine and ginger.
- Bake at 350 degrees for 30 minutes.

Juanita Messinger

Baked Pineapple

Serve as a side dish with ham.

1 tablespoon butter
2 (15-ounce) cans crushed
   pineapple
1 cup sugar
4 eggs, beaten
1/2 cup water
1/4 cup cornstarch
3 tablespoons butter,
   sliced
Cinnamon to taste

Yield: 8 servings

- Spread 1 tablespoon butter in 2-quart baking dish.
- Combine undrained pineapple, sugar and eggs in bowl; mix well. Stir in mixture of water and cornstarch. Spoon into prepared dish. Top with 3 tablespoons butter; sprinkle with cinnamon.
- Bake at 350 degrees for 1 to 1 1/2 hours or until bubbly.

Sharon West DaRe

Escalloped Pineapple

A Benander family favorite!

4 cups bread cubes, crusts
   trimmed
Milk to taste
2 cups sugar
1 cup butter, softened
3 eggs
1 (20-ounce) can crushed
   pineapple

Yield: 8 servings

- Combine bread with enough milk to moisten in bowl.
- Cream sugar and butter in mixer bowl until light and fluffy. Add eggs 1 at a time, beating well after each addition. Fold in bread and undrained pineapple.
- Spoon into baking dish sprayed with nonstick cooking spray.
- Bake at 350 degrees for 1 hour or until brown.

Gay B. Kramer

An 1896 ordinance prohibited the riding of bicycles, or any vehicles, on sidewalks at a speed more than ten miles an hour.

Macaroni Casserole

Gourmet macaroni

1 (8-ounce) package
  macaroni,
1 pound sharp Cheddar
  cheese, shredded
1 (10-ounce) can cream of
  mushroom soup
1 (4-ounce) can
  mushrooms
1 cup mayonnaise
1/4 cup chopped onion
1/4 cup chopped green bell
  pepper
1 (2-ounce) jar chopped
  pimento, drained
3 tablespoons butter
4 ounces bleu cheese
1 1/2 cups soft bread
  crumbs

Yield: 6 servings

- Cook macaroni using package directions; drain.
- Combine macaroni, Cheddar cheese, soup, undrained mushrooms, mayonnaise, onion, green pepper and pimento in bowl; mix well. Spoon into 2-quart baking dish.
- Heat butter and bleu cheese in saucepan, stirring constantly until smooth. Stir in bread crumbs. Sprinkle over macaroni mixture.
- Bake at 350 degrees for 30 minutes.

Miriam King

Aunt Lee's Macaroni Fritters

A unique blend!

1 (16-ounce) package
  elbow macaroni
1 1/4 cups freshly grated
  Parmesan cheese
1 1/4 cups freshly grated
  Romano cheese
1 1/4 cups shredded
  mozzarella cheese
1 medium onion, chopped
4 eggs, beaten
2/3 cup flour
1/3 cup milk
1 tablespoon chopped
  fresh parsley
1 teaspoon salt
1/4 teaspoon pepper
Vegetable oil for frying

Yield: 36 servings

- Cook macaroni *al dente* using package directions; drain.
- Combine macaroni, Parmesan cheese, Romano cheese, mozzarella cheese and onion in bowl; mix well. Stir in eggs, flour, milk, parsley, salt and pepper. Shape into patties, using 1/4 cup per patty.
- Fry in 1/4 inch oil in skillet over medium to medium-high heat until brown on both sides, turning once; drain.

Mary Lee Moore Bizanovich

Russian Noodles

1 (12-ounce) package
  noodles
2 cups small curd cottage
  cheese
2 cups sour cream
2 tablespoons
  Worcestershire sauce
4 to 10 drops of Tabasco
  sauce
3 bunches green onions
  with tops, chopped
8 ounces shredded
  Cheddar cheese

Yield: 8 servings

- Cook noodles using package directions;
  drain.
- Combine hot noodles with cottage cheese,
  sour cream, Worcestershire sauce, Tabasco
  sauce and green onions; mix well.
- Spoon into 9x13-inch baking dish; sprinkle
  with Cheddar cheese.
- Bake at 350 degrees for 40 minutes or until
  bubbly.

Wendy F. Hinerman

Risotto

1 onion, chopped
2 tablespoons olive oil
2 cups arborio rice
2 tablespoons olive oil
5 cups vegetable stock
3/4 cup white wine
1/4 teaspoon saffron
2/3 cup freshly grated
  Parmesan cheese

Yield: 6 servings

- Sauté onion in 2 tablespoons olive oil in
  skillet. Add rice and 2 tablespoons olive oil,
  stirring until rice is coated.
- Heat vegetable stock in saucepan. Stir in
  rice mixture.
- Simmer for 20 minutes, stirring
  occasionally. Add wine and saffron; mix
  well.
- Cook rice *al dente*. Remove from heat. Stir
  in cheese.
- May add chopped fresh basil, rosemary or
  chives, as well as leftover chicken.

Janie Altmeyer

*One hundred passenger trains were arriving and departing
daily in Wheeling in 1906. A local newspaper
announced the completion of the new railroad passenger station
in 1908 as the "B & O's Magnificent Present to Wheeling." It is now
West Virginia Northern Community College.*

Fried Rice and Peas

Great with seafood

5 tablespoons butter
3/4 cup sliced green
   onions with tops
1/3 cup finely chopped
   parsley
1 (10-ounce) package
   frozen green peas,
   thawed
4 cups cooked white or
   brown rice
2 teaspoons grated lemon
   rind
3 tablespoons soy sauce
2 dashes of Tabasco sauce

Yield: 6 servings

• Preheat wok over medium-high heat.
• Add butter. Stir in green onions and parsley.
• Stir-fry for 1 minute or until green onions are tender.
• Increase heat to high. Stir in peas, rice, lemon rind, soy sauce and Tabasco sauce.
• Stir-fry until heated through.

Doris Hastings

Garlic Rice

May be prepared 1 day in advance, refrigerated overnight and baked the day of serving

2 cups boiling water
2 teaspoons salt
1 cup long grain white rice
1/3 cup melted butter
2 tablespoons garlic salt
1 (16-ounce) can
   vegetable broth
1/2 cup slivered almonds,
   toasted
Chopped fresh parsley to
   taste

Yield: 6 servings

• Pour mixture of 2 cups boiling water and salt over rice in bowl. Let stand for 30 minutes; drain. Rinse rice; drain.
• Combine rice and butter in saucepan; mix well. Cook over medium heat for 5 minutes, stirring constantly. Stir in garlic salt and broth. Spoon into baking dish.
• Bake at 350 degrees for 45 to 60 minutes or until rice is tender. Stir in almonds and parsley.
• Bake for 10 minutes.

Janie Altmeyer

Green Rice

Pretty accompaniment to any meal

3 medium onions
2 green bell peppers
1 clove of garlic
1 cup fresh chopped
  parsley
2 cups rice, cooked
2 cups milk
2 tablespoons salt
3 eggs, beaten
1 cup shredded Cheddar
  cheese
2/3 cup vegetable oil

Yield: 8 servings

- Combine onions, green peppers, garlic and parsley in food processor container. Process until ground.
- Combine ground mixture with rice, milk, salt, eggs, cheese and oil in bowl; mix well. Spoon into baking dish.
- Bake at 350 degrees for 30 to 45 minutes or until moisture is absorbed.

Rosemary E. Miller

Rice with Chilies and Pepper Cheese

Excellent Mexican side dish

2¹/2 cups cooked rice
Salt and pepper to taste
1 teaspoon oregano
1 (4-ounce) can chopped
  green chilies
2 cups sour cream
8 ounces pepper Monterey
  Jack cheese, shredded
2 ounces Cheddar cheese,
  shredded
Paprika to taste
2 tablespoons chopped
  fresh parsley

Yield: 6 servings

- Combine rice, salt, pepper and oregano in bowl; mix well. Fold in mixture of chilies, sour cream and Jack cheese. Spoon into buttered baking dish.
- Bake at 350 degrees for 30 minutes. Sprinkle with Cheddar cheese.
- Bake until Cheddar cheese is melted. Sprinkle with paprika and parsley.

Jo Ellen Miller

In 1904, Wheeling refused Andrew Carnegie's gift of a free library. The "bloody money" was refused due to the treatment of Carnegie workers. Wheeling labor and business leaders then worked to erect a public library.

Bread
& Breakfast

WHEELING

Oglebay Institute Mansion Museum

Earl W. Oglebay purchased the former Waddington Farm mansion, built in 1846, and 25 acres of surrounding land in 1900 from his father-in-law, Andrew A. Howell. Mr. Oglebay accumulated more acreage on the hillside until, by 1905, he owned 750 acres. He landscaped the area with more than 150,000 trees and shrubs. He also created a model experimental farm, employing specialists from around the country.

Upon his death in 1926, Earl W. Oglebay willed his entire estate to the City of Wheeling, a gift the Wheeling City Council almost chose not to accept.

In 1930, Oglebay Institute was organized. It is the nation's oldest arts council. The Institute, a not-for-profit organization, has four departments: The Creative Arts Department (housed at the Stifel Fine Arts Center on National Rd.), the Mansion Museum and Glass Museum, the Nature Center, and the Performing Arts Department.

Oglebay is a 1500-acre resort. It is the only self-sustaining municipal park in operation today and it is the nation's model municipal park. It features a lodge, three golf courses, a children's zoo, an outdoor swimming pool, tennis courts, and numerous picnic sites, shelters and cabins. The annual "Winter Festival of Lights," which began in 1985, attracts over a million visitors each year. The gardens also feature a "Festival of Flowers" in the spring, summer, and early fall seasons.

photograph courtesy of Oglebay Institute Mansion Museum

Apple Breakfast Cake

3/4 cup margarine,
softened
1 1/2 cups sugar
2 eggs
2 1/4 cups flour
3/4 teaspoon baking
powder
1 teaspoon baking soda
3/4 cup milk
1 1/2 teaspoons vanilla
extract
3 medium Delicious
apples, sliced or
chopped
3/4 cup packed brown
sugar
3 tablespoons flour
3 tablespoons butter
1 teaspoon cinnamon
1 cup chopped pecans

Yield: 15 servings

- Combine margarine, sugar and eggs in mixer bowl; beat until smooth. Sift in 2 1/4 cups flour, baking powder and baking soda; mix well.
- Add milk gradually, mixing until smooth. Stir in vanilla and apples. Spoon into ungreased 9x13-inch baking pan.
- Mix brown sugar, 3 tablespoons flour, butter, cinnamon and pecans in bowl. Sprinkle over batter.
- Bake at 350 degrees for 40 to 45 minutes or until cake tests done. May serve with whipped cream. May substitute walnuts for pecans.

Gretchen Courtney Hooper

Grandma's Apple Coffee Cake

1/2 cup butter, softened
2 cups sugar
4 eggs
2 cups flour
2 teaspoons baking
powder
1/2 teaspoon salt
5 cups chopped peeled
apples
1 teaspoon vanilla extract
1 1/2 tablespoons sugar
1/2 teaspoon cinnamon

Yield: 12 servings

- Cream butter at medium speed in mixer bowl until light. Add 2 cups sugar gradually, beating constantly until fluffy. Beat in eggs 1 at a time.
- Combine flour, baking powder and salt. Add to creamed mixture; mix well. Stir in apples and vanilla.
- Spoon into greased and floured 9x13-inch baking pan. Sprinkle with mixture of 1 1/2 tablespoons sugar and cinnamon.
- Bake at 350 degrees for 45 minutes. Serve warm.

Stephanie W. Grove

Coffee Cake

1/2 cup packed brown
  sugar
1/3 cup sugar
Cinnamon to taste
1/2 cup chopped walnuts
1/2 cup butter, softened
1 cup sugar
1 tablespoon vanilla
  extract
2 eggs
2 cups sifted flour
1 teaspoon baking powder
1 teaspoon baking soda
1 cup buttermilk

Yield: 15 servings

- Mix brown sugar, 1/3 cup sugar, cinnamon and walnuts in small bowl; set aside.
- Cream butter, 1 cup sugar and vanilla in mixer bowl until light and fluffy. Beat in eggs 1 at a time, beating constantly until batter is light and smooth.
- Sift flour, baking powder and baking soda together. Add to batter 1/3 at a time, alternating with buttermilk and mixing well after each addition.
- Layer batter and walnut mixture 1/2 at a time in greased 9x13-inch baking pan. Bake at 350 degrees for 25 to 30 minutes or until coffee cake tests done.
- May substitute sour cream for buttermilk or pecans for walnuts.

Sara R. Meek

Apple Cinnamon Bread

1 1/2 cups flour
3/4 cup sugar
1 1/2 teaspoons baking soda
1/2 teaspoon cinnamon
1/2 teaspoon salt
2 eggs, beaten
1/2 cup vegetable oil
1 teaspoon vanilla extract
1 to 1 1/2 cups chopped
  apple
1 cup chopped walnuts

Yield: 12 servings

- Sift flour, sugar, baking soda, cinnamon and salt into large bowl. Add eggs, oil and vanilla; mix just until moistened.
- Fold in apple and walnuts. Spoon into greased 5x9-inch loaf pan.
- Bake at 350 degrees for 1 hour or until bread tests done. Cool in pan for 10 minutes; remove to wire rack to cool completely.

Gretchen Hooper

*Ninety percent of the metal ceilings used in the United States
were manufactured in Wheeling in 1905.*

Apricot Nut Bread

This bread has lots of apricot flavor.

1 cup chopped dried
  apricots
1 cup sugar
2 tablespoons butter
1 egg
1/2 cup orange juice
2 cups flour
2 teaspoons baking
  powder
1/4 teaspoon baking soda
1 teaspoon salt
1/2 cup chopped almonds

Yield: 12 servings

- Soak apricots in warm water to cover in bowl. Drain, reserving 1/2 cup liquid.
- Combine sugar, butter and egg in mixer bowl; mix well. Add reserved apricot liquid and orange juice.
- Mix flour, baking powder, baking soda and salt together. Add to batter; mix well. Stir in almonds and apricots. Spoon into greased and floured loaf pan.
- Bake at 350 degrees for 55 to 65 minutes or until bread tests done. Cool in pan for 10 minutes; remove to wire rack to cool completely.

Dorinda Lucas

Frosted Banana Nut Bread

2/3 cup sugar
1/3 cup shortening
2 eggs
3 tablespoons sour milk
  or buttermilk
1/2 teaspoon vanilla extract
1 cup mashed banana
2 cups flour
1 teaspoon baking powder
1/2 teaspoon baking soda
1/4 teaspoon salt
1/2 cup walnuts
2/3 cup butter
1 1/4 cups packed brown
  sugar
1/3 cup cream
Salt to taste
1 teaspoon vanilla extract
2 cups confectioners' sugar

Yield: 12 servings

- Combine sugar, shortening and eggs in mixer bowl; beat until smooth. Stir in sour milk, 1/2 teaspoon vanilla and banana.
- Sift flour, baking powder, baking soda and 1/4 teaspoon salt together. Add to batter; mix well. Stir in walnuts. Spoon into greased and floured 5x9-inch loaf pan.
- Bake at 350 degrees for 50 to 60 minutes or until loaf tests done. Cool in pan for 10 minutes; remove to wire rack to cool.
- Melt butter with brown sugar in saucepan, stirring to blend well. Boil over low heat for 2 minutes, stirring constantly; remove from heat.
- Stir in cream, pinch of salt and remaining 1 teaspoon vanilla. Cool to room temperature. Add confectioners' sugar gradually, beating constantly until creamy. Frost bread.

Samantha Hensel Buch

Monie's Cherry Bread

This bread is pretty and easy.

1 (8-ounce) bottle of
   maraschino cherries
2 eggs
1¹/₂ cups flour
2 teaspoons baking
   powder
1 cup sugar
¹/₂ cup chopped pecans

Yield: 12 servings

- Drain and chop cherries, reserving juice.
- Beat eggs in medium mixer bowl. Add flour, baking powder, sugar and pecans; mix well. Stir in cherries and reserved juice. Spoon into greased 5x9-inch loaf pan.
- Bake at 350 degrees for 1 hour. Cool in pan for 10 minutes; remove to wire rack to cool completely.

Wendy F. Hinerman

Buttermilk Chocolate Bread with Topping

¹/₂ cup margarine,
   softened
1 cup sugar
2 eggs
1 cup buttermilk
1³/₄ cups flour
¹/₂ cup baking cocoa
¹/₂ teaspoon baking
   powder
¹/₂ teaspoon baking soda
¹/₂ teaspoon salt
¹/₃ cup chopped pecans
¹/₂ cup butter, softened
2 tablespoons honey
2 tablespoons chocolate
   syrup

Yield: 12 servings

- Grease bottom of 4x8-inch or 5x9-inch loaf pan.
- Cream margarine and sugar in large mixer bowl until light and fluffy. Beat in eggs. Stir in buttermilk.
- Add flour, baking cocoa, baking powder, baking soda and salt; mix just until moistened. Stir in pecans. Spoon into prepared loaf pan.
- Bake at 350 degrees for 55 to 65 minutes or until wooden pick inserted in center comes out clean. Cool in pan for 15 minutes; remove to wire rack to cool completely.
- Combine butter, honey and chocolate syrup in small bowl; beat at high speed until light and fluffy. Store in refrigerator.
- Serve with bread.

Kathy Fortunato

The Intelligencer *newspaper paid some of the expenses for veterans to attend the 50th anniversary of the Battle of Gettysburg.*

Harvest Bread

Such a delicious fall treat!

1/2 cup butter, softened
1 cup sugar
2 eggs
13/4 cups flour
1 teaspoon baking soda
1 teaspoon cinnamon
1/2 teaspoon nutmeg
1/4 teaspoon ginger
1/4 teaspoon cloves
1/2 teaspoon salt
3/4 cup canned pumpkin
3/4 cup chocolate chips
3/4 cup chopped walnuts

Yield: 12 servings

- Cream butter and sugar in mixer bowl until light and fluffy. Beat in eggs.
- Mix next 7 ingredients together. Add to batter alternately with pumpkin, mixing constantly at slow speed. Stir in chocolate chips and walnuts. Spoon into greased 5x9-inch loaf pan.
- Bake at 350 degrees for 1 hour and 10 minutes. Cool in pan for 10 minutes; remove to wire rack to cool completely.

Ellen Brafford Valentine

Pecan Bread with Praline Glaze

1 cup raisins
1/2 cup bourbon
1 cup butter, softened
21/2 cups sugar
5 eggs
31/4 cups flour
1 teaspoon baking powder
1/2 teaspoon baking soda
11/2 teaspoons nutmeg
1 cup buttermilk
2 cups coarsely chopped
  pecans
1/2 cup packed brown
  sugar
1/4 cup sugar
1/4 cup butter
1/4 cup whipping cream
1/2 cup pecan halves

Yield: 16 servings

- Combine raisins and bourbon in bowl; mix well. Chill, covered, for 1 hour.
- Cream 1 cup butter in bowl until light. Add 21/2 cups sugar gradually, beating constantly until fluffy. Beat in eggs 1 at a time.
- Mix next 4 ingredients together. Add to creamed mixture alternately with buttermilk, beginning and ending with dry ingredients and mixing well after each addition.
- Fold in 2 cups pecans and raisin mixture. Spoon into greased and floured 10-inch tube pan.
- Bake at 325 degrees for 11/2 hours or until wooden pick inserted in center comes out clean. Cool in pan for 10 minutes; remove to wire rack to cool completely.
- Combine brown sugar, 1/4 cup sugar, 1/4 cup butter and whipping cream in heavy sauce-pan. Cook to soft-ball stage over low heat, stirring constantly. Remove from heat. Stir in pecan halves. Drizzle over cooled bread.

Renea King

Pumpkin Spice Bread

This is great served warm with whipped cream.

1/2 cup butter, softened
1 1/4 cups sugar
2 eggs
1 2/3 cups flour
1/4 teaspoon baking
  powder
1 teaspoon baking soda
1 teaspoon cinnamon
1 3/4 teaspoons ginger
1/2 teaspoon each nutmeg,
  ground cloves and salt
1 cup water
1 cup canned pumpkin
1/2 cup finely chopped
  walnuts

Yield: 12 servings

- Cream butter and sugar in mixer bowl until light and fluffy. Beat in eggs 1 at a time.
- Mix flour, baking powder, baking soda, cinnamon, ginger, nutmeg, cloves and salt together. Add to creamed mixture alternately with water, mixing well after each addition.
- Beat in pumpkin; stir in walnuts. Spoon into greased 5x9-inch loaf pan.
- Bake at 350 degrees for 1 hour. Cool in pan for 10 minutes; remove to wire rack to cool completely.
- May omit walnuts or substitute pecans for walnuts.

Mary W. Renner

Zucchini Nut Bread

2 cups unpeeled zucchini
1/2 unpeeled orange
1 cup vegetable oil
3 eggs
2 cups sugar
1 tablespoon vanilla
  extract
3 cups flour
1/4 teaspoon baking
  powder
1 teaspoon baking soda
1 tablespoon cinnamon
1 teaspoon nutmeg
1 teaspoon salt
1 cup chopped pecans

Yield: 12 servings

- Process zucchini and orange in food processor until finely grated. Combine with oil, eggs, sugar and vanilla in large bowl; mix well with spoon.
- Stir in flour, baking powder, baking soda, cinnamon, nutmeg and salt. Fold in pecans. Spoon into 2 greased 3x6-inch loaf pans.
- Bake at 325 degrees for 50 to 60 minutes or until loaves test done. Cool in pans for 10 minutes; remove to wire rack to cool completely.
- May bake in three 2x5-inch loaf pans for 35 to 40 minutes or in muffin cups for 25 minutes. May substitute other nuts for pecans.

Kathy Tannenbaum

Banana Apple Muffins

1/2 cup shortening
1 cup sugar
2 eggs
1 cup finely chopped
  peeled apple
1 cup mashed banana
1 1/2 cups flour
1 teaspoon baking soda
1/2 teaspoon salt

Yield: 24 servings

- Cream shortening in mixer bowl until light. Add sugar gradually, beating constantly until fluffy. Beat in eggs 1 at a time. Stir in apple and banana.
- Mix flour, baking soda and salt together. Add to batter; mix just until moistened.
- Spoon into paper-lined muffin cups. Bake at 350 degrees for 20 minutes.
- May add 1/4 teaspoon cinnamon, 1/2 cup raisins or 1/4 cup chopped nuts. May bake in 4 miniature loaf pans for 20 minutes if preferred.

Lisa Rae Sims

Cinnamon Puffs

1/3 cup shortening
1/2 cup sugar
1 egg
1 1/2 cups sifted flour
1 1/2 teaspoons baking
  powder
1/4 teaspoon nutmeg
1/2 teaspoon salt
1/2 cup milk
6 tablespoons melted
  butter
1/2 cup sugar
1 teaspoon cinnamon

Yield: 24 servings

- Combine shortening, 1/2 cup sugar and egg in mixer bowl; beat until smooth.
- Sift flour, baking powder, nutmeg and salt together. Add to batter alternately with milk, mixing until moistened after each addition.
- Spoon into greased or paper-lined miniature muffin cups, filling 2/3 full. Bake at 350 degrees for 15 to 20 minutes or until muffins spring back when lightly touched.
- Remove muffins from pans and paper. Dip quickly into melted butter, coat with mixture of 1/2 cup sugar and cinnamon. Cool on wire rack.

Joan Stamp

Blueberry and Peach Muffins

1³/4 cups flour
¹/2 cup sugar
2¹/2 teaspoons baking
   powder
³/4 teaspoon salt
³/4 cup milk
¹/3 cup canola oil
1 egg, beaten
³/4 cup blueberries
³/4 cup sliced peaches
2 tablespoons sugar

Yield: 12 servings

- Mix flour, ¹/2 cup sugar, baking powder and salt in large bowl; make well in center. Add milk, oil and egg to well; mix just until moistened.
- Toss blueberries and peaches with 2 tablespoons sugar in bowl. Fold gently into batter. Spoon into greased muffin cups, filling ²/3 full.
- Bake at 400 degrees for 25 minutes or until golden brown. Remove to wire rack to cool.
- May bake in miniature muffin cups for 15 to 18 minutes if preferred. May use egg substitute.

Ann Bopp

Pumpkin Miniature Muffins

1 cup canned pumpkin
¹/4 cup skim milk
2 egg whites, slightly
   beaten
¹/3 cup canola oil
1³/4 cups flour
1 cup sugar
1 tablespoon baking
   powder
2 teaspoons cinnamon
1 teaspoon each ginger
   and ground cloves
¹/4 teaspoon salt

Yield: 36 servings

- Combine pumpkin, milk, egg whites and oil in large mixer bowl; mix well.
- Mix flour, sugar, baking powder, cinnamon, ginger, cloves and salt together. Add to pumpkin mixture; mix just until moistened.
- Spoon into miniature muffin cups sprayed with nonstick canola oil, filling ³/4 full.
- Bake at 425 degrees for 10 minutes or until wooden pick inserted in muffin comes out clean. Serve warm.

Donna Niess

The 1906 Saengerfest, Wheeling and guest German singing societies, was described as Wheeling's greatest musical affair. The finale included German and American songs, with 1,500 people singing the Star Spangled Banner even though it had not yet been designated the official national anthem.

Explosion Breakfast Cake

A breakfast cake that's a big hit

1 cup flour
1 cup milk
1¹/₂ teaspoons vanilla
    extract
4 eggs
¹/₃ cup melted margarine

Yield: 10 servings

- Combine flour, milk and vanilla in blender container; process until smooth. Add eggs; process until smooth.
- Spoon into melted margarine in 9x13-inch baking pan. Bake at 425 degrees for 18 to 22 minutes or until golden brown. Serve hot with syrup.

Becky Applegate

Sunday French Toast

This is good to serve to house guests.

8 slices (³/₄-inch thick)
    French bread
4 eggs
1 cup milk
2 tablespoons Grand
    Marnier
1 tablespoon sugar
¹/₂ teaspoon vanilla extract
¹/₄ teaspoon salt
2 tablespoons margarine

Yield: 4 servings

- Arrange bread in single layer in 8x12-inch baking dish.
- Beat eggs with milk in medium mixer bowl. Add liqueur, sugar, vanilla and salt; mix well. Pour over bread. Turn bread to coat evenly.
- Chill, covered, overnight.
- Sauté bread in heated margarine in skillet for 4 minutes on each side. Garnish with confectioners' sugar.

Joan Vukelich

People mailing letters did not understand that they had to use postage stamps in addition to the "Red Cross Stamps" for Christmas in 1909. On Christmas Day the mailmen were only required to make one delivery, but they made several trips in order that no one would be disappointed.

Braided Bread

A good Easter bread

2 envelopes dry yeast
1 tablespoon sugar
1/2 cup warm water
1 cup milk
1/2 cup unsalted butter
3 eggs
2 egg yolks
7 cups flour
1 egg
1 tablespoon milk
Sesame seeds to taste

Yield: 12 servings

- Dissolve yeast and sugar in warm water in bowl. Microwave 1 cup milk in glass bowl until heated. Stir in butter.
- Combine yeast mixture, milk mixture, 3 eggs, egg yolks and 2 cups of the flour in food processor or mixer. Process or mix with dough hook until smooth. Add remaining 5 cups flour, mixing until dough forms.
- Place in greased bowl, turning to coat surface. Let rise, covered, in warm place for 2 hours or until doubled in bulk.
- Punch dough down and knead for 3 to 5 minutes or until smooth. Divide into 3 portions. Roll each portion into 18-inch rope. Braid ropes into loaf, pressing ends to seal.
- Place on baking sheet. Brush with mixture of 1 egg and 1 tablespoon milk; sprinkle with sesame seeds. Let rise, covered, for 1 hour.
- Bake at 375 degrees for 30 to 35 minutes or until golden brown. May shape into 2 smaller braids if preferred.

Samantha Hensel Buch

The 1916 Pollack Memorial Monument on Main Street was the first in the world to be dedicated to the memory of an employer of organized labor. The 37-foot-high column, with an American Eagle at the top and two union laborers shaking hands, cost $8,433.10. Walter Reuther, a Wheeling native, headed the AFL/CIO labor organization for 25 years.

Herbed Pull-Apart Bread

6 to 7 cups unbleached
  flour
2 tablespoons sugar
1 envelope dry yeast
2 teaspoons salt
1/2 cup warm milk
11/2 cups warm water
3 tablespoons butter,
  softened
3 tablespoons melted
  butter
3 large cloves of garlic,
  minced
1/2 teaspoon each
  coriander, thyme,
  marjoram and dill

Yield: 16 servings

- Combine 2 cups of the flour, sugar, yeast and salt in bowl. Mix milk, warm water and 3 tablespoons butter in small bowl. Add to yeast mixture; beat for 2 minutes.
- Add 1 cup flour; beat for 2 minutes. Add enough remaining flour to form a stiff dough, mixing well. Knead on floured surface until smooth and elastic.
- Place in oiled bowl, turning to coat surface. Let rise, covered, in warm place for 1 hour or until doubled in bulk.
- Punch dough down and divide into 2 portions. Place on floured surface; let rest for 15 minutes.
- Roll 1 portion into 8x12-inch rectangle. Brush with 11/2 tablespoons of the melted butter; sprinkle with half the garlic, coriander, thyme, marjoram and dill. Cut rectangle into four 8-inch strips. Stack strips and cut into four 2-inch squares. Stand squares, on end, down center of 1 greased loaf pan. Repeat process with remaining dough, butter, garlic and herbs in second loaf pan.
- Let rise, covered, in warm place for 1 hour. Bake at 400 degrees for 30 minutes or until golden brown. Remove to wire rack to cool.

Sally G. Riley

*The celebration for West Virginia's 50th anniversary in 1913 included
a banquet at the Scottish Rite Cathedral. The menu included
Stratford Magnesia Spring Water and Stratford Ginger Ale. One of
the events during the five day affair was an "aeroplane" six-cylinder Snyder
machine with 75-horse power which made aerial flights.*

Thick Focaccia

An Italian favorite

3¹/₂ teaspoons dry yeast
1 teaspoon sugar
1³/₄ cups lukewarm water
5¹/₂ cups bread flour
1 teaspoon salt
5 tablespoons olive oil
2 tablespoons coarse salt

Yield: 15 servings

- Combine yeast and sugar with lukewarm water in large mixer bowl; let stand for 5 minutes or until foamy. Add flour, 1 teaspoon salt and 3 tablespoons of the olive oil; knead with dough hook for 2 minutes or until mixture forms soft and sticky dough.
- Shape into a ball. Place in oiled bowl, turning to coat surface. Let rise, covered with plastic wrap, in warm place for 1¹/₂ hours or until doubled in bulk.
- Press dough into oiled 10x15-inch baking pan. Let rise for 1 hour or until nearly doubled in bulk.
- Press ¹/₄-inch deep indentations over surface of dough with fingertips. Brush with remaining 2 tablespoons olive oil; sprinkle with coarse salt.
- Bake in bottom third of 400-degree oven for 30 to 40 minutes or until golden brown. Cool slightly in pan on wire rack. Serve warm or at room temperature.
- May press dough into pan and let rise in refrigerator overnight. Let return to room temperature before proceeding.

Janie Altmeyer

During World War I, in May of 1918, the United States was raising money by the Third Liberty Loan campaign. Wheeling area bond sales were promoted by Boy Scouts, prominent citizens and local industries. The city surpassed its five million dollar goal by 1.5 million dollars. Wheeling was one of the most generous cities in the nation and was ranked 29th in over-subscription of its quota.

Cinnamon Pull-Apart Breakfast Rolls

1/2 cup sugar
1/2 cup butter
1 teaspoon salt
1 cup boiling water
1 envelope dry yeast
1/4 cup warm water
2 eggs, beaten
41/2 cups bread flour
3/4 cup melted butter
11/2 cups sugar
1 tablespoon cinnamon

Yield: 12 servings

- Place 1/2 cup sugar, 1/2 cup butter and salt in bowl. Add boiling water, stirring to melt butter. Cool to lukewarm.
- Dissolve yeast in lukewarm water in small bowl. Add to butter mixture. Beat in eggs. Add flour, mixing to form soft dough. Chill, covered, overnight.
- Let dough stand at room temperature for 30 minutes. Mix 3/4 cup butter, 11/2 cups sugar and cinnamon in bowl.
- Shape dough into 11/2-inch balls. Coat with cinnamon mixture; arrange in tube pan.
- Bake at 375 degrees for 45 to 50 minutes or until light brown. Invert onto serving plate.

Sarah H. Koeniger

Cinnamon Twists

These are a traditional Sunday breakfast treat!

1 cup sour cream
1/4 cup sugar
1/8 teaspoon baking soda
1 teaspoon salt
1 cake yeast
1 egg
2 tablespoons shortening
3 cups flour
2 tablespoons butter,
    softened
1/2 cup packed brown
    sugar
11/2 teaspoons cinnamon

Yield: 24 servings

- Warm sour cream in saucepan; remove from heat. Stir in sugar, baking soda and salt. Crumble yeast over mixture; mix gently. Let stand until dissolved. Add egg, shortening and flour; mix well to form dough.
- Knead dough several times on floured surface. Roll into 6x24-inch rectangle. Spread with butter; sprinkle brown sugar and cinnamon lengthwise over half the dough.
- Fold other half of dough over to cover brown sugar mixture. Cut into 24 one-inch strips. Twist strips; place on greased baking sheet, pressing ends to baking sheet.
- Let rise, covered, for 1 hour. Bake at 375 degrees for 12 to 15 minutes or until golden brown. Serve warm.

Pat Hensel

Dinner Rolls

2 envelopes yeast
¹/₄ cup lukewarm water
¹/₂ cup milk
¹/₂ cup sugar
1 teaspoon vanilla extract
1 teaspoon salt
3¹/₂ cups flour
2 eggs

Yield: 18 servings

- Soften yeast in lukewarm water in small bowl.
- Scald milk in saucepan. Combine with sugar, vanilla and salt in bowl. Add enough flour to make thick batter. Add yeast and eggs; beat with spoon to mix well. Stir in remaining flour.
- Knead on floured surface for 10 minutes. Place in greased bowl, turning to coat surface. Let rise, covered, in warm place for 1¹/₂ hours or until nearly doubled in bulk.
- Punch dough down. Shape as desired; place in baking pan. Let rise until doubled in bulk. Bake at 350 degrees until golden brown.

Virginia C. England

Bessie's Bran Refrigerator Rolls

1 cup shortening
³/₄ cup sugar
1 cup bran cereal
1¹/₂ teaspoons salt
1 cup boiling water
2 eggs, beaten
2 cakes yeast, crumbled
1 cup lukewarm water
5¹/₂ to 6¹/₂ cups flour
6 tablespoons butter,
  softened

Yield: 36 servings

- Combine shortening, sugar, cereal and salt in large bowl. Stir in boiling water. Cool to room temperature. Stir in eggs.
- Dissolve yeast in lukewarm water in small bowl. Add to cereal mixture with half the flour; mix well. Add enough remaining flour to form a soft dough; mix well.
- Let rise in refrigerator overnight.
- Roll into 3 circles on floured surface. Spread with butter. Cut each circle into 12 wedges. Roll up wedges from wide end and shape into crescents; place on baking sheet. Let rise until doubled in bulk.
- Bake at 425 degrees for 15 minutes.

Pat Hensel

M-m-m-m Good Bread Spread

1 cup butter, softened
1 pound Swiss cheese,
    shredded
1/4 cup chopped green
    onions
2 tablespoons mustard
2 tablespoons poppy seeds
1 loaf French or Italian
    bread, thinly sliced

Yield: 32 servings

- Combine butter, cheese, green onions, mustard and poppy seeds in bowl; mix well. Spread on bread slices.
- Place on baking sheet. Bake at 350 degrees until cheese melts. May spread on crackers to use as appetizer.

Anne Clark

Julie's Garlic Bread

Just add a salad for a full meal.

6 tablespoons mayonnaise
1/2 cup butter, softened
1/2 teaspoon minced garlic
3/4 cup grated Parmesan
    cheese
2 tablespoons chopped
    parsley
1/2 teaspoon oregano
1 loaf Italian bread

Yield: 8 servings

- Combine mayonnaise, butter, garlic, cheese, parsley and oregano in bowl; mix well. Cut bread horizontally into halves. Spread cut sides with butter mixture.
- Place bread halves together; wrap with foil. Place on baking sheet.
- Bake at 350 degrees for 20 minutes. Open halves of loaf. Bake for 5 minutes longer.

Gay B. Kramer

Granola Bars

1/2 cup packed brown
    sugar
1/3 cup margarine,
    softened
1/3 cup peanut butter
1/4 cup dark corn syrup
1 egg
1 cup raisins
1/2 cup chocolate chips
3 cups rolled oats
1/2 teaspoon vanilla extract
1/4 teaspoon cinnamon

Yield: 18 servings

- Mix brown sugar, margarine, peanut butter and corn syrup in mixer bowl until smooth. Beat in egg. Add raisins, chocolate chips, oats, vanilla and cinnamon; mix well.
- Press into 9x9-inch baking pan. Bake at 350 degrees for 25 to 30 minutes or until set. Cool on wire rack. Cut into bars.
- May omit chocolate chips or substitute pecans for chocolate chips.

Angela Ceo

Breakfast Casserole

1 pound sausage
1/4 cup chopped onion
1/4 cup chopped green bell
  pepper
6 eggs
1/2 cup sour cream
Pepper to taste

Yield: 6 servings

- Brown sausage with onion and green pepper in skillet, stirring until sausage is crumbly; drain. Spread 3/4 of the mixture in medium baking dish.
- Combine eggs, sour cream and pepper in bowl; mix well. Spoon over sausage.
- Bake at 350 degrees until egg mixture is soft-set; mix well. Top with remaining sausage mixture. Bake for total of 45 minutes or until firm.

Pam Lacefield

Brunch Casserole

1 (8-count) can crescent
  rolls
1 pound pork sausage
2 cups shredded
  mozzarella cheese
4 eggs, beaten
3/4 cup milk
1/4 teaspoon salt
1/8 teaspoon pepper

Yield: 8 servings

- Place roll dough in 9x13-inch buttered baking pan, pressing edges and perforations to seal.
- Brown sausage in medium skillet, stirring until crumbly; drain. Layer sausage and cheese in prepared pan.
- Combine eggs, milk, salt and pepper in bowl; mix well. Spoon over layers.
- Bake at 425 degrees for 15 minutes or until set. Let stand for 5 minutes. Cut into squares.

Renea King

Stifel and Sons provided textiles to the Belgian and French governments and khaki for the American doughboys during World War I.

Breakfast Pizza

1 package refrigerator
  pizza dough
1 pound sausage
1/2 cup sliced mushrooms
1/2 cup chopped green bell
  pepper
1/2 cup chopped onion
1 cup shredded Cheddar
  cheese
1 cup shredded
  mozzarella cheese
5 eggs
1/3 cup water

Yield: 6 servings

• Press pizza dough into 13-inch pizza pan.
• Brown sausage in skillet, stirring until crumbly; drain. Sprinkle over dough. Layer mushrooms, green pepper, onion and cheeses over sausage. Chill, covered, overnight if desired.
• Combine eggs and water in bowl; mix well. Pour over layers.
• Bake at 350 degrees for 15 minutes or until eggs are set and cheese is melted.
• May substitute ground beef for sausage or use vegetable topping of your choice.

Mariann Price

Green Chili Eggs

1 (4-ounce) can chopped
  green chilies
6 to 8 ounces Monterey
  Jack cheese, shredded
12 eggs
4 ounces sour cream
4 ounces plain yogurt

Yield: 8 servings

• Layer green chilies and cheese in greased 9x13-inch baking dish. Beat eggs with sour cream and yogurt in bowl. Pour over layers.
• Bake at 350 degrees for 30 minutes or until set. Garnish with sliced tomatoes and fresh cilantro.
• May use egg substitute if preferred.

Becky Raimonde

*Wheeling's American Legion Post No. 1 is
the first post in the country.*

Quiche

8 ounces cooked ham,
  chopped
1 cup shredded Swiss
  cheese
1/3 cup chopped onion
1/2 cup baking mix
2 cups milk
4 eggs
Salt and pepper to taste

Yield: 6 servings

- Layer ham, cheese and onion in pie plate.
  Combine baking mix, milk, eggs, salt and
  pepper in blender container; process until
  smooth. Pour over layers.
- Bake at 350 degrees for 40 minutes or until
  set. Cut into wedges.

Beth Ann Dague

Savory Sausage Strudels

1 pound hot sausage
1 pound mild sausage
2 pounds mushrooms,
  chopped
1 medium onion, chopped
2 tablespoons butter
16 ounces cream cheese,
  softened
1 package frozen puff
  pastry, thawed

Yield: 8 servings

- Cook sausage in skillet, stirring until
  crumbly; drain. Sauté mushrooms and
  onion in butter in small skillet. Add to
  sausage. Stir in cream cheese.
- Place sheet of pastry on work surface.
  Spread with half the sausage mixture. Roll
  up pastry to enclose filling. Place seam side
  down on baking sheet. Repeat with
  remaining pastry and sausage mixture.
- Bake at 400 degrees for 20 minutes. May
  prepare in advance and freeze. Bake frozen
  strudel at 450 degrees for 10 minutes and at
  400 degrees for 1 hour longer.

Gretchen Courtney Hooper

Cookies & Candy

WHEELING

First Capitol of West Virginia

In 1814, the oldest independent school west of the Alleghenies was founded with a bequest left by Wheeling attorney Noah Linsly. The school was originally called the Lancastrian Academy and later became Linsly Institute.

Linsly Institute was located on the northwest corner of 15th and Eoff streets. This building was built in 1859. When the state of West Virginia was formed in 1863, Linsly leased this building to the new state for use as the capitol. Wheeling was the capital of West Virginia from 1863 to 1870 and again from 1875 to 1885.

Linsly School operates today as a private coeducational preparatory academy. It is located in the Leatherwood area of Wheeling.

Blonde Brownies

2 cups flour
1 teaspoon baking powder
1 teaspoon baking soda
1 teaspoon salt
1 cup chopped pecans
1 cup butter
2 cups packed brown
  sugar
2 eggs, beaten
1 teaspoon vanilla extract
2 cups semisweet
  chocolate chips

Yield: 32 servings

• Sift flour, baking powder, baking soda and
  salt into bowl. Add pecans; mix well.
• Melt butter in saucepan; remove from heat.
  Add brown sugar; blend well. Let stand
  until cool.
• Add eggs and vanilla; mix well. Add flour
  mixture gradually, mixing well after each
  addition.
• Spread evenly in 9x13-inch greased baking
  pan. Sprinkle chocolate chips over top.
• Bake at 350 degrees for 35 minutes. Cool.
  Cut into squares.

Joan T. Grubler

Caramel Squares

Grandma Balch's recipe

1/4 cup butter
1 cup packed brown sugar
1 egg, beaten
3/4 cup flour
1 teaspoon baking powder
1/2 teaspoon vanilla extract
1/2 cup chopped pecans

Yield: 16 servings

• Combine butter and brown sugar in
  saucepan; mix well. Cook until blended,
  stirring constantly.
• Stir a small amount of hot mixture into egg;
  stir egg into hot mixture. Cook until heated
  through, stirring constantly.
• Stir in flour and baking powder. Add vanilla
  and pecans; mix well. Spread in ungreased
  8x8-inch baking pan.
• Bake at 350 degrees for 30 minutes. Cool.
  Cut into squares.

Wendy F. Hinerman

Chocolate Cherry Bombs

1 cup margarine, softened
2 cups sugar
2 eggs
1 tablespoon vanilla
  extract
3 cups flour
1/2 teaspoon baking soda
1/2 teaspoon salt
1/2 teaspoon baking
  powder
1 cup baking cocoa
48 maraschino cherry
  halves
1 (14-ounce) can
  sweetened condensed
  milk
2 cups chocolate chips
1 tablespoon maraschino
  cherry juice

Yield: 48 servings

- Cream margarine, sugar, eggs and vanilla in mixer bowl until light and fluffy. Add mixture of flour, baking soda, salt, baking powder and cocoa; mix well.
- Shape into 1-inch balls. Place on ungreased cookie sheet.
- Bake at 350 degrees for 12 minutes. Press cherry half into center of each cookie. Remove to wire rack.
- Combine condensed milk, chocolate chips and cherry juice in double boiler. Cook over hot water until smooth, stirring constantly.
- Frost warm cookies with chocolate mixture.

Jo Ellen Miller

Chocolate Mint Brownies

Add to your Christmas cookie list

1/2 cup margarine, softened
1 cup sugar
2 eggs
3 egg whites
1 cup flour
1 teaspoon vanilla extract
1/4 teaspoon salt
1 (16-ounce) can
  chocolate syrup
1/2 cup margarine,
  softened
1 1/2 tablespoons milk
2 cups confectioners' sugar
1 teaspoon peppermint
  extract
3 drops of green food
  coloring
1/2 cup margarine
2 cups chocolate chips

Yield: 60 servings

- Cream 1/2 cup margarine, sugar, eggs, egg whites, flour, vanilla, salt and chocolate syrup in mixer bowl until smooth. Spread in greased 10x15-inch baking sheet.
- Bake at 350 degrees for 25 minutes. Cool completely.
- Beat 1/2 cup margarine, milk, confectioners' sugar, peppermint extract and green food coloring in mixer bowl until light and fluffy. Spread over baked layer.
- Chill for 1 hour.
- Combine 1/2 cup margarine and chocolate chips in saucepan. Cook until blended, stirring constantly. Spread over chilled layers.
- Chill in refrigerator. Cut into squares.

Sarah L. Gompers

Coconut and Almond Brownies

1 cup whole almonds
2 tablespoons butter,
  softened
3 ounces cream cheese,
  softened
1/4 cup sugar
1 egg, beaten
1 tablespoon flour
1²/3 cups flaked coconut
5 ounces semisweet
  chocolate
1/4 cup butter
1/2 cup sugar
1/2 teaspoon vanilla extract
2 eggs, beaten
1/2 cup flour
1/2 teaspoon baking
  powder
1/4 teaspoon salt
1 ounce semisweet
  chocolate, melted

Yield: 16 servings

- Reserve 16 whole almonds. Chop remaining almonds.
- Cream 2 tablespoons butter and cream cheese in mixer bowl until light and fluffy. Beat in 1/4 cup sugar. Stir in 1 egg, 1 tablespoon flour and coconut. Add 1/3 cup chopped almonds; mix well.
- Combine 5 ounces chocolate and 1/4 cup butter in saucepan. Cook over low heat until smooth, stirring constantly. Remove from heat.
- Stir in 1/2 cup sugar and vanilla. Add 2 eggs; mix well. Stir in 1/2 cup flour, baking powder and salt. Add remaining chopped almonds; mix well.
- Spread chocolate mixture in greased 8x8-inch baking pan. Top with cream cheese mixture. Sprinkle with reserved almonds.
- Bake at 350 degrees for 40 minutes or until edges pull from sides of pan. Drizzle with 1 ounce melted chocolate.
- Cool in pan. Cut into squares.

Vera Barton-Caro

Chocolate Kiss Brownies

1 cup butter
2 cups semisweet
  chocolate chips
1¹/3 cups sugar
1 teaspoon vanilla extract
4 eggs
1 cup flour
1 cup chopped pecans
48 chocolate kisses

Yield: 48 servings

- Melt butter and chocolate chips in double boiler over boiling water, stirring constantly until smooth. Remove from heat.
- Stir in sugar and vanilla. Add eggs 1 at a time, mixing well after each addition. Stir in flour and pecans.
- Fill foil liners in miniature muffin cups 3/4 full.
- Bake at 350 degrees for 20 to 25 minutes or until brownies test done. Press chocolate kiss into center of each brownie.
- Remove to wire rack to cool

Robyn Ruttenberg

Worth-A-Mint Brownies

These brownies are great as a simple, but festive, after-dinner dessert with coffee.

1/2 cup margarine,
  softened
1 cup sugar
2 eggs
1 teaspoon vanilla extract
1/2 teaspoon peppermint
  extract
2/3 cup flour
1/2 cup baking cocoa
1/2 teaspoon baking
  powder
1/4 teaspoon salt
3 tablespoons melted
  margarine
1/2 cup baking cocoa
1 1/2 cups confectioners'
  sugar
2 tablespoons milk
1/2 teaspoon vanilla extract
1/4 teaspoon peppermint
  extract
1 tablespoon milk
10 peppermint starlight
  mints, crushed

Yield: 16 servings

- Cream 1/2 cup margarine, sugar, eggs, 1 teaspoon vanilla and 1/2 teaspoon peppermint extract in mixer bowl until smooth. Stir in sifted mixture of flour, 1/2 cup cocoa, baking powder and salt. Spread in 8x8-inch baking pan.
- Bake at 350 degrees for 20 to 25 minutes or until edges pull from sides of pan.
- Remove to wire rack to cool.
- Combine 3 tablespoons melted margarine and 1/2 cup cocoa in mixer bowl; mix well. Add confectioners' sugar, 2 tablespoons milk, 1/2 teaspoon vanilla and 1/4 teaspoon peppermint extract, beating until creamy. Add 1 tablespoon milk gradually, beating until of spreading consistency.
- Frost baked layer; sprinkle with crushed peppermint mints. Cut into squares.

Laura Phillips Miller

Deluxe Chocolate Chip Cookies

2/3 cup shortening
2/3 cup butter, softened
1 cup sugar
1 cup packed light brown
  sugar
2 eggs
2 teaspoons vanilla extract
3 1/2 cups flour
1 teaspoon baking soda
1 teaspoon salt
1 cup chopped macadamia
  nuts
2 cups semisweet
  chocolate chips

Yield: 60 servings

- Cream shortening, butter, sugar, brown sugar, eggs and vanilla in mixer bowl until light and fluffy.
- Stir in flour, baking soda, salt, macadamia nuts and chocolate chips. Drop by rounded tablespoonfuls 2 inches apart on ungreased cookie sheet.
- Bake at 375 degrees for 8 to 10 minutes or until edges are light brown.
- Cool slightly. Remove to wire rack to cool completely.

Brenda G. Moore

Italian Chocolate Cookies

5 cups flour
2 cups sugar
¾ cup baking cocoa
1 tablespoon cinnamon
2 tablespoons baking
   powder
2 teaspoons cloves
1 cup shortening
¾ cup milk
5 eggs, beaten
1 cup chopped pecans

Yield: 90 servings

- Combine flour, sugar, cocoa, cinnamon, baking powder and cloves in bowl; mix well. Cut in shortening until crumbly. Add milk, eggs and pecans; mix well.
- Shape into 1-inch balls. Place on greased cookie sheet.
- Bake at 350 degrees for 10 to 15 minutes or until browned. Remove to wire rack to cool.
- Frost with different colored icings of your choice.

Victoria Gompers

French Galettes (Pizzeles)

Do not drive after licking bowl!

1 (16-ounce) package
   light brown sugar
2 cups sugar
12 eggs, slightly beaten
2 cups butter, softened
6 shots of whiskey
¼ cup vanilla extract
6 cups sifted flour
1 (⅛-ounce) bottle of
   anise oil

Yield: 120 servings

- Sift brown sugar and sugar together in large bowl; mix well. Stir in eggs.
- Add butter, whiskey, vanilla, flour and anise oil; mix well
- Spoon batter onto hot pizzele iron. Bake using manufacturer's directions. Remove to wire rack to cool.
- May substitute brandy for whiskey.

Beth R. Weaver

Charles A. Lindbergh visited Wheeling ten weeks after he was the first person to fly alone across the Atlantic Ocean in 1927.

Gingersnaps

Handed down from mother to daughter

¹/₃ cup sugar
²/₃ cup packed brown
　sugar
³/₄ cup shortening
1 egg, beaten
1 teaspoon cinnamon
1 teaspoon ground cloves
1 teaspoon ginger
2 teaspoons baking soda
2 cups flour
¹/₄ teaspoon salt
¹/₂ cup sugar

Yield: 36 servings

- Cream ¹/₃ cup sugar, brown sugar, shortening and egg in mixer bowl until light and fluffy. Stir in cinnamon, cloves, ginger, baking soda, flour and salt. Chill, covered, in refrigerator.
- Shape into 1-inch balls; roll in ¹/₂ cup sugar. Place 2 inches apart on ungreased cookie sheet.
- Bake at 350 degrees for 10 to 15 minutes or until light brown.
- Remove to wire rack to cool.

Margie Ball

Holiday Nuggets

¹/₄ cup butter
¹/₂ cup confectioners'
　sugar
³/₄ cup shortening
1 tablespoon vanilla
　extract
1 teaspoon almond extract
¹/₂ cup chopped pecans
2 cups sifted flour
¹/₂ teaspoon salt
¹/₂ cup confectioners'
　sugar

Yield: 36 servings

- Cream butter, ¹/₂ cup confectioners' sugar and shortening in mixer bowl until light and fluffy. Stir in flavorings and pecans.
- Add sifted mixture of flour and salt gradually; mix well. Shape by tablespoonfuls into small balls. Place on ungreased cookie sheet; flatten slightly.
- Bake at 325 degrees for 25 minutes. Roll hot cookies in ¹/₂ cup confectioners' sugar. Remove to wire rack to cool.
- May roll in mixture of confectioners' sugar and colored sugar.

Margie Ball

A majestic statue of The Aviator was unveiled on Armistice Day in 1925 at Linsly School. Five Army planes in a breathtaking sham battle were part of the dedication.

Lemon Cheese Bars

1 (2-layer) package yellow
 cake mix with pudding
1 egg
1/3 cup canola oil
8 ounces light cream
 cheese, softened
1/3 cup sugar
1 teaspoon lemon juice
1 egg

Yield: 24 servings

- Combine cake mix, 1 egg and canola oil in bowl, stirring until crumbly. Reserve 1 cup crumb mixture.
- Press remaining crumb mixture into ungreased 9x13-inch baking pan.
- Bake at 350 degrees for 15 minutes.
- Beat cream cheese, sugar, lemon juice and 1 egg in mixer bowl until smooth. Spread over baked layer. Sprinkle with reserved crumb mixture.
- Bake for 15 minutes. Cool. Cut into bars.

Donna Niess

Pecan Diamonds

Tastes like mini pecan pies!

1/2 cup chilled margarine
11/2 cups flour
1/4 cup ice water
11/2 cups packed light
 brown sugar
1 cup butter
1/2 cup honey
1/3 cup sugar
1 pound pecan pieces or
 halves
1/4 cup whipping cream

Yield: 50 servings

- Cut margarine into flour until crumbly. Add ice water, tossing lightly with fork. Shape into a ball; wrap in plastic wrap.
- Chill for 1 hour.
- Roll dough into 10x14-inch rectangle on lightly floured surface. Fit into buttered and floured 9x13-inch baking pan; dough will come halfway up sides. Pierce with fork. Chill.
- Bring brown sugar, butter, honey and sugar to a boil in saucepan, stirring constantly.
- Boil for 4 minutes or until thickened, stirring constantly. Remove from heat. Stir in pecans and whipping cream. Pour over chilled layer.
- Bake at 375 degrees for 25 minutes or until edges are brown. Cool in pan.
- Cut lengthwise into 1-inch strips; cut diagonally into 1-inch strips to create diamond shapes.

Diana J. Davis

Peanut Butter Bars

1 cup peanut butter
2/3 cup margarine,
   softened
1 teaspoon vanilla extract
2 cups packed brown
   sugar
3 eggs
1 cup flour
1/2 teaspoon salt
3/4 cup confectioners'
   sugar
2 teaspoons water
1/4 cup semisweet
   chocolate chips
1 teaspoon shortening

Yield: 36 servings

- Beat peanut butter, margarine and vanilla in mixer bowl until smooth. Add brown sugar, beating until light and fluffy. Beat in eggs until blended.
- Stir in flour and salt. Spread in greased 9x13-inch baking pan.
- Bake at 350 degrees for 30 to 35 minutes or until edges pull from sides of pan. Cool slightly.
- Combine confectioners' sugar and water in bowl; drizzle over warm layer.
- Combine chocolate chips and shortening in double boiler. Cook over hot water until smooth, stirring constantly. Drizzle over warm layer.
- Cool. Cut into bars.

Julie Squibb

Pumpkin Cookies

1 cup sugar
1 cup shortening
1 egg
1 cup cooked pumpkin
1 teaspoon vanilla extract
2 cups flour
1 teaspoon baking powder
1 teaspoon baking soda
1 teaspoon cinnamon
1/2 teaspoon salt
1/2 cup packed brown
   sugar
3 tablespoons butter
4 teaspoons milk
1 cup confectioners' sugar

Yield: 36 servings

- Beat sugar, shortening, egg, pumpkin and vanilla in mixer bowl until blended. Stir in flour, baking powder, baking soda, cinnamon and salt.
- Drop by teaspoonfuls onto ungreased cookie sheet.
- Bake at 375 degrees for 12 to 15 minutes or until brown. Remove to wire rack to cool.
- Combine brown sugar, butter and milk in saucepan. Cook for 2 minutes, stirring constantly. Cool. Stir in confectioners' sugar. May add additional milk if needed for desired consistency. Frost tops of cookies with icing.
- May add 1 cup chopped nuts and 1 cup raisins to batter.

Brenda Thomas

No-Bake Chocolate Cookies

2 cups sugar
1/2 cup whole milk
1/2 cup margarine
1/2 cup baking cocoa
1 cup shredded coconut
1/2 cup peanut butter
1 teaspoon vanilla extract
3 cups quick-cooking oats

Yield: 36 servings

- Bring sugar, milk, margarine and cocoa to a boil in saucepan. Boil for 1 minute. Remove from heat.
- Stir in coconut, peanut butter and vanilla. Add oats 1 cup at a time, mixing well after each addition.
- Drop by spoonfuls onto waxed paper.

Gay B. Kramer

No-Bake Chocolate Peanut Butter Bars

2 cups graham cracker crumbs
3 1/2 cups confectioners' sugar
1 cup melted margarine
1 teaspoon vanilla extract
2 cups chocolate chips
1 cup peanut butter

Yield: 36 servings

- Combine graham cracker crumbs, confectioners' sugar, melted margarine and vanilla in bowl; mix well. Pat into 9x13-inch glass dish.
- Combine chocolate chips and peanut butter in double boiler. Cook over hot water until smooth. Spread over prepared layer.
- Cool. Cut into bars.

Jane Krupica

Glazed Almonds

1/2 cup whole almonds
1/2 cup sugar
2 tablespoons butter
1/2 teaspoon vanilla
Salt to taste

Yield: 4 servings

- Combine almonds, sugar and butter in heavy skillet.
- Cook over medium heat for 15 minutes or until almonds are toasted and glaze is brown, stirring constantly. Stir in vanilla.
- Spread almonds on foil; sprinkle lightly with salt.
- Cool. Break into clusters.

Suzy Haning

Candied Pecans

3 tablespoons butter
¼ cup packed brown
  sugar
1 cup pecan halves
Salt to taste

Yield: 8 servings

- Combine butter and brown sugar in heavy skillet. Cook over medium heat until bubbly, stirring constantly.
- Add pecans, stirring until coated.
- Spread pecans in shallow baking pan. Broil 5 inches from heat source for 1 minute or until pecans are toasted. Sprinkle lightly with salt.

Ella Jane Howard

Buckeyes

1 (16-ounce) package
  confectioners' sugar
1½ cups peanut butter
1 cup margarine, softened
1 teaspoon maple extract
Confectioners' sugar to
  taste
12 ounces semisweet
  chocolate
10 to 12 teaspoons melted
  paraffin

Yield: 100 servings

- Beat 16 ounces confectioners' sugar, peanut butter, margarine and maple extract in mixer bowl until smooth.
- Dust hands with confectioners' sugar. Shape dough into small balls. Place on waxed paper-lined cookie sheets. Chill until firm.
- Melt chocolate in double boiler over hot water. Stir in paraffin.
- Dip chilled candy balls partially into chocolate mixture to resemble buckeyes.
- Chill until set.

Janet Kropp

The third annual Christmas Parade, in 1933, was sponsored by the Wheeling Chamber of Commerce. Santa Claus, with his sleigh and live reindeer, was the main attraction. Unemployed men were given a dollar to wear a "mummer's costume" and march in the parade.

Christmas Caramels

4 cups whipping cream
2 cups milk
2 pounds sugar
2 cups light corn syrup

Yield: 72 servings

- Combine whipping cream and milk in pitcher; mix well.
- Combine sugar, corn syrup and 2 cups of cream mixture in 6-quart saucepan.
- Cook over medium heat to 238 degrees on candy thermometer, stirring constantly with wooden spoon. Stir in 2 cups of cream mixture.
- Cook over medium heat to 238 degrees on candy thermometer, stirring constantly with wooden spoon. Stir in remaining cream mixture.
- Cook over medium heat to 238 degrees on candy thermometer, stirring constantly with wooden spoon.
- Pour onto buttered cookie sheet. Cool. Cut into small squares. Wrap individually with waxed paper or plastic wrap.
- May substitute 6 cups half and half for cream mixture.

Robert C. Miller

Microwave Caramel Corn

16 cups air-popped popcorn
1 cup packed brown sugar
1/4 cup corn syrup
1/2 cup margarine
1/2 teaspoon salt
1/2 teaspoon baking soda

Yield: 16 servings

- Place popcorn in large brown paper grocery bag.
- Combine brown sugar, corn syrup, margarine and salt in large microwave-safe bowl. Microwave on High for 1 1/2 minutes or until mixture boils. Boil for 3 minutes. Remove from microwave. Add baking soda, stirring until foamy. Pour over popcorn.
- Fasten bag loosely. Microwave on High for 2 minutes, shaking bag after 1 minute. Microwave on High for 30 seconds; shake bag.
- Pour popcorn onto greased baking sheet. Cool.

Sherri K. Kellas

Chocolate Raspberry Truffles

The league members request this recipe.

1¹/₃ cups semisweet
   chocolate chips
2 tablespoons whipping
   cream
1 tablespoon butter
2 tablespoons seedless
   raspberry jam
1 to 2 cups chocolate chips
Confectioners' sugar to
   taste

Yield: 50 servings

- Combine 1¹/₃ cups chocolate chips, cream and butter in double boiler. Cook over hot water until smooth, stirring constantly. Stir in jam.
- Freeze, covered with plastic wrap, for 20 minutes.
- Shape into balls. Place on cookie sheet. Freeze until firm.
- Melt 1 to 2 cups chocolate chips in double boiler over hot water, stirring occasionally.
- Using wooden pick, dip candy balls 1 at a time into chocolate. Place on cookie sheet.
- Chill until set. Dust with confectioners' sugar.

Janie Altmeyer

Coconut Bonbons

A big hit with coffee after dinner

1 cup light corn syrup
1 (14-ounce) package
   coconut
2 teaspoons orange extract
50 almonds
1 to 2 cups semisweet
   chocolate chips

Yield: 50 servings

- Place corn syrup in microwave-safe dish. Microwave for 2¹/₂ to 3 minutes or until of thin consistency. Stir in coconut and orange extract.
- Chill, covered, for 1 hour.
- Shape into small balls with moist hands. Place on waxed paper-lined cookie sheet. Place almond inside each ball.
- Chill in refrigerator.
- Melt chocolate in double boiler over hot water. Dip candy balls into chocolate. Place on waxed paper-lined surface or in paper bonbon cups. Let stand until set.
- Store in airtight container.

Samantha Hensel Buch

Coconut Date Balls

1 pound dates, chopped
2 eggs, beaten
1 teaspoon vanilla extract
1 cup sugar
3 tablespoons butter
1 cup chopped pecans
3 cups crisp rice cereal
2 cups shredded coconut

Yield: 60 servings

- Combine dates, eggs, vanilla, sugar and butter in saucepan; mix well.
- Cook over medium heat for 7 minutes or until thickened, stirring constantly. Remove from heat. Stir in pecans and cereal.
- Drop by teaspoonfuls into coconut in bowl; shape into small balls. Coat with coconut.

Cynthia L. Reasbeck

Peanut Brittle

1 cup peanuts
1/8 teaspoon baking soda
2 cups sugar
1/8 teaspoon salt
1 teaspoon butter

Yield: 16 servings

- Grease baking sheet. Place in warm oven.
- Combine peanuts and baking soda in bowl, tossing to coat.
- Combine sugar, salt and butter in large skillet. Cook over medium heat until sugar melts, stirring constantly.
- Add peanuts, tossing to coat. Spread in thin layer on prepared baking sheet.
- Cool. Break into pieces.

Kathy Tannenbaum

The Ohio River is owned by the state of West Virginia within the state's boundaries. The river system carries more commodities than any other river in the nation and exceeds the annual tonnage which passes through the Panama Canal.

Tiger Butter

1 pound white chocolate
1 (12-ounce) jar chunky
  peanut butter
1 pound semisweet
  chocolate, melted

Yield: 50 servings

- Combine white chocolate and peanut butter in microwave-safe dish. Microwave on Low until blended, stirring occasionally.
- Spread in 3-quart dish or 9x13-inch dish sprayed with nonstick cooking spray.
- Swirl semisweet chocolate into white chocolate mixture with knife.
- Chill until set. Cut into squares.

Emily S. Fisher

Irresistible Taffy

It is fun to have a taffy-pull party, especially for teenagers.

4 cups sugar
1/2 cup vinegar
1 cup water
Vanilla extract to taste

Yield: 32 servings

- Combine sugar, vinegar and water in saucepan; mix well. Cook over low heat to 250 to 268 degrees on candy thermometer, hard-ball stage.
- Pour into large buttered pan. Sprinkle generously with vanilla.
- Let stand until edges are cool. Scrape edges into center of pan until mixture is cool enough to handle.
- Pull off a piece at a time, pulling until taffy is opaque and elastic with satin finish. Wrap each piece in waxed paper.

Janet Kropp

Desserts

W H E E L I N G

Monument Place

Monument Place, also known as the Osiris Temple, is the oldest-known building in Ohio County, dating to 1798. The house, called Shepherd Hall by its owners, Moses and Lydia Shepherd, was constructed from stone quarried from the banks of Wheeling Creek. The building is in the Federal style, and was luxurious by frontier standards. It had seven rooms, including a ballroom which runs the center five windows of the second story. It is in this ballroom that Lydia played hostess to such illustrious people as Henry Clay, the Marquis de Lafayette, John C. Calhoun, Andrew Jackson, James K. Polk, Zachary Taylor, Thomas Hart Benton, and Daniel Webster.

Local lore claims that Wheeling was chosen to become the terminus for the National Road because of Lydia's great feminine charms. Moses was awarded the contract from the Pennsylvania line to the Ohio River in Wheeling. He added two extra bridges in order that the highway would pass by his home. One of these bridges is still in use at the intersection of Route 88 and Route 40 in Elm Grove. The circa 1817 "Hump Bridge" is the oldest extant bridge in West Virginia.

Monuments on the property gave rise to the name "Monument Place." These included a sundial in memory of Moses Shepherd and a huge monument honoring Henry Clay.

Additions have been made to both sides of the mansion and dormer windows were added on the third story. The current owner, the Osiris Shrine Temple A.A.O.N.M.S., added on to the rear of the mansion in the 1950s.

photograph courtesy of Beverly B. Fluty

Baklava

12 ounces butter, cut into
  1/4-inch pieces
1/2 cup vegetable oil
40 (12x16-inch) sheets
  frozen phyllo dough,
  thawed (2 boxes)
4 cups chopped walnuts
3 cups sugar
1 1/2 cups water
2 tablespoons fresh lemon
  juice

Yield: 36 servings

- Melt butter in heavy saucepan over low heat. Heat until foamy but not brown, skimming off foam; remove from heat. Let stand for 2 to 3 minutes. Spoon off clarified butter; discard solids.
- Combine oil and clarified butter in bowl. Spread about 1 tablespoon of the mixture over bottom and sides of 9x13-inch baking pan.
- Fold 1 sheet phyllo dough in half. Place in pan and open dough; fold edges in to fit pan. Brush with butter mixture. Add another sheet of dough and brush with butter mixture. Sprinkle with 3 tablespoons of the walnuts.
- Repeat process to make 19 layers. Top with remaining 2 layers phyllo; brush with remaining butter mixture. Score layers into diamonds at 2-inch intervals, cutting 1/2 inch deep.
- Bake on middle oven rack at 350 degrees for 30 minutes. Reduce oven temperature to 300 degrees. Bake for 45 minutes longer or until crisp and golden brown.
- Combine sugar, water and lemon juice in small saucepan. Cook over medium heat until sugar dissolves and mixture boils, stirring constantly. Increase heat to high.
- Cook for 5 minutes or to 220 degrees on candy thermometer. Pour over baked layer.
- Cool to room temperature. Cut into diamond shapes.

Nermin D. Lavapies

Apple Cobbler

You may substitute peaches for apples in this dish.

1 cup sugar
3 tablespoons flour
1/4 teaspoon cinnamon
Salt to taste
5 cups sliced peeled
   apples
Juice of 1 orange
2 tablespoons butter
1 cup flour
1 cup sugar
1 teaspoon baking powder
3/4 teaspoon salt
1 egg
1 tablespoon grated
   orange rind
1/3 cup melted butter
Cinnamon to taste

Yield: 8 servings

- Mix 1 cup sugar, 3 tablespoons flour, 1/4 teaspoon cinnamon and salt to taste in large bowl. Toss apples with orange juice in medium bowl. Add to cinnamon mixture; toss gently to coat well.
- Arrange apples in ungreased 9x13-inch baking dish; dot with 2 tablespoons butter.
- Combine 1 cup flour, 1 cup sugar, baking powder and 3/4 teaspoon salt in bowl; mix well. Add egg; mix with pastry blender until crumbly. Mix in orange rind. Sprinkle evenly over apples. Drizzle with 1/3 cup melted butter; sprinkle with cinnamon to taste.
- Bake at 350 degrees for 35 to 40 minutes or until golden brown. Serve with whipped cream or vanilla ice cream.

Helen Kubisiak

Berry Crumble

This is a great summer dessert for a small dinner party.

2 pints fresh blueberries
1/4 cup lemon juice
1/3 cup packed dark brown
   sugar
1/4 cup flour
2 tablespoons butter
Cinnamon and salt to taste

Yield: 6 servings

- Toss blueberries with lemon juice in bowl. Spoon into buttered 2-quart baking dish.
- Combine brown sugar and flour in bowl. Cut in butter until crumbly. Stir in cinnamon and salt. Sprinkle over blueberries.
- Bake at 375 degrees for 15 minutes or until bubbly. Serve with whipped cream or ice cream.

Linda Gompers

Boiled Custard

This recipe was a specialty of my mother, Virginia. She often made it for friends recovering from illnesses.

1 quart milk
2 eggs
2 egg yolks
1 cup sugar
1 tablespoon vanilla
   extract
2 egg whites

Yield: 6 servings

- Scald milk in double boiler over hot water.
- Beat eggs and egg yolks in bowl. Add sugar; mix well. Add scalded milk; mix well.
- Strain mixture into double boiler. Cook over hot water until thickened, stirring constantly. Stir in vanilla. Cool to room temperature.
- Beat egg whites in mixer bowl until stiff peaks form. Fold gently into custard.

Mary Eleanor Colvin

Delicious Cherry Torte

4 egg whites
1/2 cup sugar
1/2 cup packed brown
   sugar
25 butter crackers,
   crushed
1 1/2 cups chopped pecans
8 ounces cream cheese,
   softened
2 teaspoons milk
1 cup confectioners' sugar
1 tablespoon sugar
12 ounces whipped
   topping
1 (21-ounce) can cherry
   pie filling

Yield: 12 servings

- Beat egg whites in mixer bowl until soft peaks form. Add 1/2 cup sugar and brown sugar, beating until stiff peaks form. Stir in cracker crumbs and pecans. Spread in 9x13-inch baking dish.
- Bake at 350 degrees for 20 minutes; do not overbake. Cool to room temperature.
- Combine cream cheese, milk and confectioners' sugar in bowl; mix well. Spread over baked layer; sprinkle with 1 tablespoon sugar.
- Layer whipped topping over top. Dip cherries 1 at a time from pie filling and arrange over dessert. Spoon cherry filling over top. Chill until serving time.

Jane Krupica

Chocolate Mousse

1/2 cup coffee
1/2 cup sugar
2 cups chocolate chips
4 extra-large eggs,
  separated
1/8 teaspoon cream of
  tartar
3/4 cup sugar
3 cups whipping cream,
  whipped
1 (8-ounce) package
  chocolate wafers,
  crushed

Yield: 12 servings

- Mix coffee and 1/2 cup sugar in saucepan. Cook over medium heat until sugar dissolves. Reduce heat to low. Stir in chocolate chips until melted; remove from heat; cool slightly.
- Beat in egg yolks 1 at a time. Cool completely.
- Beat egg whites in mixer bowl until foamy. Add cream of tartar; beat until soft peaks form. Add 3/4 cup sugar, beating at medium speed until smooth. Beat at high speed until stiff but not dry.
- Fold half the chocolate mixture into egg whites; fold egg whites into remaining chocolate mixture. Fold in whipped cream.
- Spoon into large glass bowl or soufflé dish. Sprinkle with wafer crumbs. Chill until serving time.
- May prepare in advance and freeze for up to 2 weeks.

Patricia M. Cullinane

Amaretto Cheesecake

1 1/2 cups vanilla wafer
  crumbs
6 tablespoons melted
  margarine
1/3 cup sugar
1/2 cup chopped almonds
1/2 cup chopped pecans
Salt to taste
24 ounces cream cheese,
  softened
1 (14-ounce) can
  sweetened condensed
  milk
3 eggs
1 teaspoon sugar
1 teaspoon almond extract
1/3 cup Amaretto

Yield: 12 servings

- Combine vanilla wafer crumbs, margarine, 1/3 cup sugar, almonds, pecans and salt in bowl; mix well. Pat into 9-inch springform pan.
- Beat cream cheese and condensed milk in mixer bowl until smooth. Add eggs, 1 teaspoon sugar, almond extract and Amaretto, beating until blended.
- Spoon blended mixture over prepared layer.
- Bake at 350 degrees for 1 hour. Cool on wire rack for 30 minutes. Chill for 3 to 4 hours.

Cookbook Committee

Fluffy Cheesecake

2 cups graham cracker
   crumbs
1/2 cup sugar
1/2 cup melted butter
6 egg yolks
16 ounces cream cheese,
   softened
1 cup sugar
2 tablespoons flour
2 teaspoons vanilla extract
6 egg whites, stiffly beaten
2 cups sour cream
1/2 cup sugar
2 teaspoons vanilla extract

Yield: 24 servings

- Mix graham cracker crumbs, 1/2 cup sugar
   and butter in bowl; mix well. Press into
   9x13-inch baking dish.
- Beat egg yolks in mixer bowl until thick and
   lemon-colored. Add cream cheese; beat at
   medium speed until smooth. Add 1 cup
   sugar, flour and 2 teaspoons vanilla; mix
   well at medium speed.
- Fold in egg whites. Pour into prepared dish.
- Bake at 350 degrees for 30 minutes. Cool on
   wire rack for 10 minutes.
- Blend sour cream, 1/2 cup sugar and 2
   teaspoons vanilla with spoon in bowl.
   Spread over cheesecake.
- Bake for 10 minutes longer. Serve warm or
   chilled.

Becky Applegate

Chocolate Chip Cheesecake

1 1/2 cups chocolate wafer
   crumbs
1 tablespoon sugar
3 tablespoons melted
   butter
16 ounces cream cheese,
   cubed, softened
1 cup sugar
4 eggs
2 teaspoons vanilla extract
3/4 cup miniature
   semisweet chocolate
   chips

Yield: 10 servings

- Mix cookie crumbs, 1 tablespoon sugar and
   melted butter in bowl. Press over bottom
   and 1 inch up side of 8-inch springform pan.
- Combine cream cheese, 1 cup sugar, eggs
   and vanilla in mixer bowl; mix until
   smooth. Spoon into prepared pan. Sprinkle
   with chocolate chips.
- Bake at 325 degrees for 1 hour and 10
   minutes to 1 hour and 15 minutes or until
   wooden pick inserted in center comes out
   clean.
- Cool on wire rack. Chill for 6 hours or
   longer. Loosen cake from side of pan with
   knife; place on serving plate. Remove side
   of pan.

Suzy Q. Member

Praline Cheesecake

1 cup vanilla wafer crumbs
2 tablespoons sugar
1/4 cup butter, softened
1 1/2 cups chopped pecans
3 tablespoons butter,
  softened
24 ounces cream cheese,
  softened
1 cup packed dark brown
  sugar
2 tablespoons flour
3 eggs
2 teaspoons vanilla extract
1 cup chopped pecans
1/4 cup packed dark brown
  sugar
1 1/2 teaspoons sugar
2 tablespoons whipping
  cream
1 tablespoon butter
1/2 teaspoon vanilla extract

Yield: 12 servings

- Combine vanilla wafer crumbs, 2 tablespoons sugar and 1/4 cup butter in bowl; mix well. Press into 9-inch springform pan. Chill in refrigerator.
- Combine 1/2 cup of the pecans and 3 tablespoons butter on baking sheet. Toast at 350 degrees until golden brown. Cool to room temperature. Reduce oven temperature to 325 degrees.
- Combine cream cheese, 1 cup brown sugar and flour in mixer bowl; beat until light and fluffy. Beat in eggs 1 at a time. Stir in 2 teaspoons vanilla and remaining 1 cup pecans. Pour into prepared crust.
- Bake for 1 hour. Turn off oven and open oven door. Let cheesecake stand in oven for 30 minutes. Cool to room temperature. Place on serving plate; remove side of pan.
- Combine 1/4 cup brown sugar, 1 1/2 teaspoons sugar, cream and 1 tablespoon butter in small saucepan. Bring to a boil, stirring to dissolve sugar. Cook over low heat to 225 degrees on candy thermometer; remove from heat. Cool slightly. Stir in 1/2 teaspoon vanilla.
- Sprinkle toasted pecans over cheesecake; drizzle with praline sauce. Chill for 6 to 8 hours.

Wendy F. Hinerman

*Oglebay Institute, organized in 1930, is the nation's oldest arts council.
The annual Winter Festival of Lights, which began
in 1985, attracts over a million visitors each year to Oglebay.*

Chocolate Mousse Cake with Whipped Cream

7 ounces bittersweet
   chocolate
1/2 cup unsalted butter
7 egg yolks
3/4 cup sugar
1 teaspoon vanilla extract
7 egg whites
1/8 teaspoon cream of
   tartar
1/4 cup sugar
1 cup whipping cream
1/2 cup confectioners'
   sugar
1 teaspoon vanilla extract

Yield: 10 servings

- Melt chocolate with butter in double boiler over hot water over low heat.
- Beat egg yolks with 3/4 cup sugar in large mixer bowl for 5 minutes or until very thick and lemon-colored. Beat in chocolate mixture and 1 teaspoon vanilla.
- Beat egg whites with cream of tartar in mixer bowl until soft peaks form. Add 1/4 cup sugar 1 tablespoon at a time, beating constantly until stiff peaks form. Fold gently into egg yolk mixture.
- Spread 3/4 of the mixture into ungreased 9-inch springform pan. Cover remaining mixture; chill in refrigerator.
- Bake at 325 degrees for 35 minutes. Cool on wire rack; center will fall. Place on serving plate; remove side of pan.
- Stir chilled chocolate mixture until smooth. Spread over top. Chill until firm.
- Whip cream in mixer bowl until soft peaks form. Add confectioners' sugar and 1 teaspoon vanilla; beat until smooth. Spread over top and side of mousse cake. Chill for several hours to overnight. Garnish with chocolate shavings.

Robyn Ruttenberg

Waddington Gardens is a spectacular display of Mother Nature's finest.
The Gardens cover the hilltop region of Oglebay surrounding the
Mansion Museum and recreate many of the gardens of old Waddington Farm.
Springtime brings brilliant tulips, daffodils, and flowering trees. June
through September brings an awesome array of annual flowers and dozens of
hanging baskets. With the arrival of fall, the Gardens become
filled with brilliant chrysanthemums.

Chocolate and Almond Gâteau

1 cup semisweet
  chocolate chips
2/3 cup butter
3/4 cup sugar
3 egg yolks
3/4 cup flour
1 1/2 teaspoons vanilla
  extract
1/2 teaspoon salt
1/4 cup milk
2/3 cup toasted sliced
  almonds
3 egg whites
3 tablespoons butter
2 tablespoons light corn
  syrup
1 tablespoon water
1 cup semisweet
  chocolate chips

Yield: 10 servings

- Melt 1 cup chocolate chips in double boiler over hot water, stirring until smooth.
- Combine 2/3 cup butter and sugar in mixer bowl; beat until smooth. Beat in melted chocolate, egg yolks, flour, vanilla and salt. Add milk gradually, beating constantly until smooth. Stir in almonds.
- Beat egg whites in mixer bowl until stiff peaks form. Fold in chocolate mixture. Spread in greased springform pan.
- Bake at 350 degrees for 25 to 30 minutes or until set. Cool in pan for 10 minutes. Place on wire rack; remove side of pan. Cool completely.
- Combine 3 tablespoons butter, corn syrup and water in small saucepan. Bring to a boil over low heat; remove from heat. Stir in 1 cup chocolate chips. Cool to lukewarm.
- Spoon over gâteau. Cut into wedges.

Virginia C. England

Heath Bar Dessert

1 (2-layer) package
  chocolate cake mix
1 (8-ounce) jar
  butterscotch caramel
  sauce
6 (1 1/2-ounce) Heath bars,
  crushed
12 ounces whipped
  topping
2 ounces milk chocolate,
  shaved

Yield: 15 servings

- Prepare and bake cake mix using package directions for 9x13-inch baking pan. Pierce 5 rows of holes in cake with straw.
- Spread caramel sauce over cake; sprinkle with candy. Spread with whipped topping. Top with chocolate shavings. Chill until serving time.
- Note: For best results use butterscotch caramel topping, not plain butterscotch.

Janie Altmeyer

Chocolate Overdose

1 package brownie mix
1 (4-ounce) package
  chocolate pudding mix
2 (1½-ounce) chocolate
  candy bars, crumbled
1 (12-ounce) jar hot fudge
  sauce
8 ounces chocolate
  whipped topping
¼ cup chocolate sprinkles

Yield: 8 servings

• Prepare brownie mix using package
  directions for 9x13-inch baking pan. Cool
  on wire rack. Cut into small pieces.
• Prepare chocolate pudding mix using
  package directions.
• Layer half the brownies, pudding,
  remaining brownies, candy, hot fudge sauce,
  whipped topping and sprinkles in large
  bowl. Chill until serving time.

Ellen Brafford Valentine

Chocolate Kahlua Trifle

1 (2-layer) package yellow
  cake mix
½ cup semisweet
  chocolate chips
3 (4-ounce) packages
  chocolate instant
  pudding mix
3 cups cold milk
½ cup Kahlua
12 ounces whipped
  topping

Yield: 12 servings

• Prepare and bake cake mix using package
  directions for 9x13-inch cake pan and
  adding chocolate chips to batter. Cool on
  wire rack. Crumble cake.
• Mix pudding mix with cold milk in bowl.
• Layer cake, Kahlua, pudding and whipped
  topping ⅓ at a time in trifle bowl, pressing
  cake layers down firmly. Swirl topping;
  garnish with chocolate shavings.
• Chill, covered, for 2 hours or longer.

Lisa Rae Sims

Wheeling's Italian heritage is brought to life every year in July.
The Upper Ohio Valley Italian Festival features bocce tournaments, wine
tasting, cultural exhibits, dancing, morra games, and the true flavor
of Italy. The three-day event is held on the streets of downtown Wheeling.

Chocolate Raspberry Truffle Torte

2 (10-ounce) packages
  frozen raspberries
1 pound unsalted butter,
  cut into tablespoons
1 cup sugar
12 ounces semisweet
  chocolate, coarsely
  chopped
4 ounces bittersweet
  chocolate, coarsely
  chopped
1/2 cup Chambord or
  raspberry brandy
1/2 teaspoon raspberry
  extract
8 eggs, at room
  temperature
2/3 cup whipping cream
8 ounces bittersweet
  chocolate, finely
  chopped
2 tablespoons unsalted
  butter, softened
16 fresh raspberries

Yield: 16 servings

- Butter bottom and side of 3x10-inch cake pan; line bottom with waxed paper. Strain raspberries, reserving 1/2 cup juice.
- Combine 1 pound butter, sugar, semisweet chocolate and 4 ounces bittersweet chocolate in double boiler. Cook over hot water until sugar dissolves, stirring until mixture is smooth; remove from heat.
- Stir in liqueur, reserved raspberry juice and raspberry extract. Whisk in eggs 1 at a time. Stir in strained raspberries. Spoon into prepared baking pan. Place in larger pan with water to halfway up the cake pan.
- Bake at 325 degrees for 1 hour to 1 hour and 10 minutes or until wooden pick inserted in center comes out clean. Cool on wire rack for 2 to 3 hours or until room temperature.
- Chill, covered with plastic wrap, for 3 hours to overnight.
- Combine cream, 8 ounces bittersweet chocolate and 2 tablespoons butter in double boiler. Cook over hot water until chocolate and butter melt, stirring to mix well.
- Cover chocolate mixture with plastic wrap. Chill for 30 to 45 minutes or until thickened to pudding consistency, stirring occasionally.
- Loosen side of cake from pan with knife; invert onto serving plate and remove waxed paper. Reserve 3/4 cup chilled chocolate mixture. Spread remaining chilled chocolate mixture over top and side of torte.
- Pipe reserved chilled chocolate mixture into 16 rosettes on torte using pastry bag fitted with star tip. Arrange fresh raspberries on top of torte. Chill until serving time

Janie Altmeyer

Chocolate Sundae Cake

1 (2-layer) package
  chocolate cake mix
1 (14-ounce) can
  sweetened condensed
  milk
1 (12-ounce) can
  chocolate syrup
1/2 cup crushed walnuts
1/2 cup chopped
  maraschino cherries

Yield: 15 servings

- Prepare and bake chocolate cake using package directions for 9x13-inch baking pan.
- Pierce cake with knife. Pour condensed milk and chocolate syrup over cake; sprinkle with walnuts and cherries.
- Chill until serving time.

Nermin D. Lavapies

French Vanilla Ice Cream with Fudge Sauce

1 cup sugar
2 tablespoons flour
1/8 teaspoon salt
2 cups half and half
2 eggs, at room
  temperature, beaten
2 cups whipping cream
1 1/2 teaspoons vanilla
  extract
Fudge Sauce

Yield: 12 servings

- Combine sugar, flour and salt in double boiler. Add half and half gradually. Cook over hot water for 10 to 15 minutes or until sugar dissolves and mixture thickens, stirring constantly.
- Whisk a small amount of hot mixture into beaten egg yolks; whisk egg yolks into hot mixture. Cook for 1 minute, stirring constantly. Chill. Stir in cream and vanilla. Spoon into ice cream freezer container. Chill until time to freeze.
- Freeze using manufacturer's instructions. Serve with hot Fudge Sauce.

Fudge Sauce

1 cup sugar
1/3 cup baking cocoa
2 tablespoons flour
1/4 teaspoon salt
1 cup boiling water
1 tablespoon butter
1/2 teaspoon vanilla extract

Yield: 12 servings

- Combine sugar, cocoa, flour, salt and boiling water in saucepan. Cook over low heat until of desired consistency, stirring occasionally. Add butter and vanilla.

Beth Ann Dague

Cream Puff Supreme

1 cup water
1/2 cup butter
1 cup flour
4 eggs
2 (4-ounce) packages
   vanilla instant pudding
   mix
3 1/2 cups milk
8 ounces cream cheese,
   softened
12 ounces whipped
   topping
1/2 cup chocolate syrup

Yield: 12 servings

- Bring water to a boil in saucepan. Stir in butter until melted; remove from heat. Add flour; mix well. Add eggs 1 at a time, mixing well after each addition.
- Spread mixture in lightly greased 9x13-inch baking pan. Bake at 425 degrees for 10 minutes. Reduce oven temperature to 350 degrees. Bake for 20 minutes longer. Cool to room temperature.
- Combine pudding mix, milk and cream cheese in mixer bowl; mix until smooth. Spread over baked layer. Top with whipped topping; drizzle with chocolate syrup.

Nini Zadrozny

Lemon Tiramisu

1/4 cup fresh lemon juice
3 tablespoons
   confectioners' sugar
1/3 cup cream sherry
2 (3-ounce) packages
   ladyfingers, split
1 cup whipping cream
1/4 cup confectioners'
   sugar
8 ounces mascarpone
   cheese
1/4 cup confectioners'
   sugar
1 teaspoon lemon extract
1 tablespoon grated lemon
   rind
1 (10-ounce) jar lemon
   curd
1/2 cup lemon yogurt

Yield: 8 servings

- Blend lemon juice and 3 tablespoons confectioners' sugar in bowl. Stir in wine. Brush mixture over bottom and side of glass bowl. Brush cut sides of ladyfingers with mixture. Arrange some of the ladyfingers cut side in over bottom and side of prepared bowl.
- Beat cream in large mixer bowl until soft peaks form. Beat in 1/4 cup confectioners' sugar.
- Beat cheese at medium speed in mixer bowl until smooth. Add 1/4 cup confectioners' sugar and lemon extract gradually, beating constantly until light and fluffy. Fold in lemon rind and whipped cream.
- Combine lemon curd and yogurt in mixer bowl; beat at medium speed until light and fluffy.
- Layer lemon curd mixture, cheese mixture and remaining ladyfingers 1/2 at a time in prepared bowl. Chill, covered, for 6 hours to overnight.

Janie Altmeyer

Bread Pudding with Brandy Sauce

1 quart milk
10 slices day-old bread,
  torn
1 cup light cream
4 eggs
1 cup sugar
1/4 cup melted margarine
1/2 cup golden raisins
1/2 teaspoon nutmeg
1 teaspoon cinnamon
1 teaspoon vanilla extract
Brandy Sauce

Yield: 8 servings

- Heat milk in saucepan. Combine with bread and cream in large bowl; mix well.
- Beat eggs slightly in medium bowl. Stir in sugar. Add to bread mixture with margarine, raisins, nutmeg, cinnamon and vanilla; mix well.
- Spoon into buttered shallow 2-quart baking dish. Place in larger pan with 1 inch hot water. Bake at 350 degrees for 1 hour or until knife inserted in center comes out clean.
- Serve warm with Brandy Sauce.

Brandy Sauce

3 egg yolks
1 cup sugar
1 1/2 cups milk
1 teaspoon vanilla extract
1 1/2 tablespoons
  cornstarch
1/4 cup water
6 tablespoons brandy

Yield: 8 servings

- Beat egg yolks slightly in small saucepan. Add sugar, milk and vanilla; mix well. Bring to a boil over low heat, stirring constantly.
- Stir in mixture of cornstarch and water. Cook until thickened, stirring constantly; remove from heat. Stir in brandy. Serve warm or chilled.

Joan Vukelich

*Carriage House Glass Center in Oglebay features an historic glass museum.
Visitors are also treated to demonstrations of glass blowing and glass
decorating. The Carriage House Gift Shop features the largest selection
of West Virginia glass products and other unique glass items. One popular
item is a twelve-inch replica of the famous Sweeney punch bowl.*

Crème Brûlée with Raspberries

This is absolutely sublime.

1 (12-ounce) package
  frozen unsweetened
  raspberries, thawed,
  drained
1/4 cup sugar
5 egg yolks
1/2 cup sugar
2 cups whipping cream
Vanilla extract to taste
5 tablespoons unsalted
  butter
5 tablespoons brown sugar

Yield: 6 servings

- Toss raspberries gently with 1/4 cup sugar in bowl. Divide evenly between six 3/4-cup ramekins or custard cups.
- Whisk egg yolks and 1/2 cup sugar in heavy saucepan for 3 minutes or until thick and lemon-colored. Add cream and vanilla. Cook over medium heat for 7 minutes or until mixture coats back of spoon, stirring constantly; do not boil. Stir in butter until melted.
- Spoon custard over raspberries in custard cups. Chill, covered, for 4 hours to overnight.
- Press brown sugar through fine sieve onto tops of custard. Broil in preheated broiler for 2 minutes or until sugar begins to caramelize. Chill for 3 hours.

Mary W. Renner

Grape Nut Pudding

If you like Grape Nuts, you will love this Cape Cod favorite!

2 cups milk
1 tablespoon butter
1/2 cup Grape Nuts cereal
2 eggs
1/2 cup sugar
1 teaspoon vanilla extract

Yield: 4 servings

- Scald mixture of milk, butter and Grape Nuts in saucepan.
- Beat eggs in mixer bowl. Add sugar and vanilla; mix well. Stir a small amount of hot mixture into eggs; stir eggs into hot mixture.
- Spoon into greased small baking dish; place in larger pan with 1 inch hot water. Bake at 350 degrees for 1 hour or until knife inserted in center comes out clean.

Holly Joseph

Vanilla Mousse with Butterscotch Rum Sauce

3 envelopes unflavored
   gelatin
1 cup sugar
1/2 teaspoon salt
4 cups milk
2 tablespoons plus 1
   teaspoon vanilla extract
4 cups whipping cream,
   whipped
Butterscotch Rum Sauce

Yield: 12 servings

- Mix gelatin, sugar and salt in medium saucepan. Stir in milk gradually. Let stand for several minutes or until gelatin is softened. Bring to a boil over medium heat, stirring to dissolve gelatin completely.
- Combine with vanilla in bowl; mix well. Place bowl in larger bowl of ice water. Stir until mixture cools and thickens.
- Fold in whipped cream. Spoon into lightly greased 12-cup mold. Chill, covered with plastic wrap, for 3 hours or longer.
- Loosen mousse from side of mold with knife; dip mold into warm water. Unmold onto large platter. Drizzle with warm Butterscotch Rum Sauce.

Butterscotch Rum Sauce

2/3 cup light corn syrup
1/4 cup unsalted butter
11/4 cups packed light
   brown sugar
21/2 tablespoons dark rum
1/3 cup milk

Yield: 12 servings

- Combine corn syrup, butter, brown sugar and rum in medium saucepan. Bring to a boil over medium heat. Cook to 236 degrees on candy thermometer, soft-ball stage; remove from heat.
- Stir in milk. Heat to serving temperature over low heat. May thin with additional rum, milk or cream if sauce becomes too thick. May substitute half and half for milk.

Donna Glass

Wheeling Downs, located on historic Wheeling Island, features greyhound racing. The multilevel complex offers a variety of viewing areas for the exciting finish-line action.

English Trifle

3 tablespoons cornstarch
2 tablespoons sugar
2 eggs
1 quart milk
4 teaspoons almond
  extract
8 ladyfingers
12 almond macaroons
1 (8-ounce) jar raspberry
  jam
2 cups whipping cream
2 tablespoons sugar
2 teaspoons almond
  extract
1/2 cup honey-roasted
  almonds

Yield: 8 servings

- Whisk cornstarch, 2 tablespoons sugar and eggs in saucepan. Whisk in milk and 4 teaspoons almond extract. Cook over low heat until thickened, whisking constantly.
- Break each ladyfinger and macaroon into 4 or 5 pieces. Spread each piece with jam. Sprinkle into 8 dessert dishes.
- Spoon custard into prepared dessert dishes. Chill, covered, overnight.
- Whip cream in mixer bowl until frothy. Add 2 tablespoons sugar and 2 teaspoons almond extract, beating constantly until soft peaks form. Spoon onto custard in dessert dishes; top with almonds.
- May substitute toasted and salted slivered almonds for honey-roasted almonds.

Shirley W. Weaver

Almond-Crusted Pound Cake

1 cup sliced almonds
1 (16-ounce) package
  golden pound cake
1/2 teaspoon almond
  extract

Yield: 12 servings

- Press half the almonds over bottom and 2/3 up sides of generously greased 5x9-inch loaf pan.
- Prepare cake using package directions, adding almond extract. Spoon into prepared pan. Sprinkle with remaining almonds.
- Bake at 325 degrees for 40 to 50 minutes or until cake tests done. Cool in pan for 10 minutes; remove to wire rack to cool completely. Serve with strawberries and whipped cream.
- May substitute white cake mix with pound cake recipe on package if unable to find pound cake mix.

Linda Gompers

Fresh Apple Cake

1¹/₄ cups canola oil
2 cups sugar
2 eggs
2 teaspoons vanilla extract
3 cups unbleached flour
1 teaspoon baking soda
1 teaspoon cinnamon
1 teaspoon nutmeg
¹/₂ cup chopped walnuts
¹/₂ cup raisins
3 cups sliced tart apples

Yield: 12 servings

- Combine oil, sugar, eggs and vanilla in mixer bowl; mix well. Mix flour, baking soda, cinnamon and nutmeg together. Fold into oil mixture.
- Stir in walnuts, raisins and apples. Spoon into greased 9x13-inch cake pan.
- Bake at 350 degrees for 15 minutes. Reduce temperature to 325 degrees. Bake for additional 35 to 40 minutes or until cake tests done. Serve warm with vanilla ice cream.

Ange Lavy Joel

Banana Blueberry Cake

1³/₄ cups sugar
1¹/₄ cups vegetable oil
2 cups mashed bananas
2 cups flour
1 tablespoon baking powder
¹/₂ teaspoon baking soda
¹/₂ teaspoon salt
1 teaspoon vanilla extract
4 eggs
1 cup sour cream
2 cups chopped walnuts
2 cups blueberries

Yield: 12 servings

- Combine sugar, oil and bananas in large mixer bowl; mix at low speed. Add flour, baking powder, baking soda, salt, vanilla, eggs and sour cream; mix well. Fold in walnuts and blueberries.
- Spoon into greased and floured 10-inch tube pan. Bake at 350 degrees for 1 hour to 1 hour and 10 minutes or until wooden pick inserted in center comes out clean.
- Cool in pan for 10 minutes; remove to wire rack to cool completely. Garnish with confectioners' sugar.

Diana I. Ihlenfeld

Super Moist Banana Cake

3/4 cup shortening
2 1/4 cups sugar
1 1/2 teaspoons vanilla
    extract
3 eggs
3 cups flour
1 teaspoon baking powder
1 teaspoon baking soda
3/4 teaspoon salt
1/3 cup buttermilk
1 1/2 cups mashed bananas

Yield: 16 servings

- Cream shortening in mixer bowl until light. Add sugar gradually, beating until fluffy. Beat in vanilla and eggs.
- Mix next 4 ingredients together. Add to egg mixture alternately with buttermilk, mixing well after each addition. Stir in bananas.
- Spoon into 3 greased and floured 9-inch cake pans. Bake at 350 degrees for 30 minutes or until wooden pick inserted in center comes out clean. Cool in pans for 10 minutes; remove to wire rack to cool completely.
- May fill layers with butterscotch pudding and frost with butter frosting.

Caryn Buch

Grandma G's Banana Cake

This has been our traditional family birthday cake for years. The special flavor cannot be achieved with a packaged mix.

2 cups sifted flour
1 teaspoon baking powder
1 teaspoon baking soda
1 teaspoon salt
1/2 cup shortening
1 1/2 cups sugar
1 egg, beaten
1 cup mashed bananas
3/4 cup sour milk
1 teaspoon vanilla extract
1 egg white
1 cup packed brown sugar
2 tablespoons water
Salt to taste
1 teaspoon vanilla extract

Yield: 12 servings

- Sift flour, baking powder, baking soda and salt together 3 times.
- Cream shortening and sugar in mixer bowl until light and fluffy. Beat in egg and bananas. Add dry ingredients alternately with sour milk, mixing well after each addition. Mix in 1 teaspoon vanilla.
- Spoon into greased and floured 9x13-inch cake pan. Bake at 350 degrees for 30 minutes or at 375 degrees for 25 minutes. Cool on wire rack.
- Combine egg white, brown sugar, water and salt in double boiler. Cook over hot water, beating constantly at high speed for 5 minutes or until stiff peaks form. Beat in 1 teaspoon vanilla. Spread over cake.

Judi Tarowsky

Card Club Chocolate Chip Cake

1 (4-ounce) package
  chocolate pudding and
  pie filling mix
1 (2-layer) package
  chocolate cake mix
1 cup chocolate chips

Yield: 15 servings

- Prepare pudding mix using package directions. Cool. Stir in cake mix.
- Spoon mixture into greased and floured 9x13-inch cake pan. Sprinkle with chocolate chips.
- Bake at 350 degrees for 25 to 30 minutes or until edges pull from sides of pan. Remove to wire rack to cool.

Kathy Parsons

Carrot Cake

2 cups sugar
1¹/2 cups vegetable oil
4 eggs, beaten
2 cups flour
2 teaspoons baking soda
2 teaspoons baking
  powder
2 teaspoons cinnamon
1 teaspoon salt
1 cup chopped pecans
3 cups grated carrots
8 ounces cream cheese,
  softened
1/4 cup butter, softened
1 (16-ounce) package
  confectioners' sugar
2 teaspoons vanilla extract
1/2 cup chopped pecans

Yield: 12 servings

- Combine sugar and oil in bowl; mix well. Stir in eggs. Add mixture of flour, baking soda, baking powder, cinnamon and salt; mix well.
- Stir in 1 cup pecans and carrots. Spoon into 3 greased 9-inch cake pans.
- Bake at 325 degrees for 30 minutes or until layers test done. Remove to wire rack to cool.
- Beat cream cheese, butter and confectioners' sugar in mixer bowl until smooth. Stir in vanilla. Fold in 1/2 cup pecans.
- Spread frosting between layers and over top and side of cake.
- May bake in two 9-inch cake pans for 35 to 40 minutes.

Cookbook Committee

Speidel Championship Course is listed in Golf Digest's top 75 public courses. The golf course was designed by Robert Trent Jones.

Low-Fat Chocolate Cake

2 cups (scant) sugar
3/4 cup applesauce
4 egg whites
1/2 cup coffee
2 1/2 cups flour
1 cup boiling water
1 1/2 teaspoons baking
    powder
1/2 cup baking cocoa
1 teaspoon baking soda

Yield: 16 servings

- Combine sugar, applesauce, egg whites, coffee, flour, boiling water and baking powder in large mixer bowl. Add cocoa and baking soda dissolved in a small amount of warm water; mix well.
- Spoon into greased and floured bundt pan. Bake at 350 degrees for 25 to 35 minutes or until wooden pick inserted in center comes out clean. Cool in pan on wire rack for 15 minutes; remove to rack to cool completely.
- Garnish cake with confectioners' sugar and slivered almonds.

Barbara Whitehead

Chocolate Zucchini Cake

This makes a moist rich chocolate cake that does not need frosting.

9 tablespoons butter,
    softened
2 cups sugar
3 (1-ounce) squares
    unsweetened chocolate
    or 3 ounces premelted
    chocolate
3 eggs
1/2 cup milk
2 cups coarsely grated
    unpeeled zucchini
2 teaspoons grated orange
    rind
2 teaspoons vanilla extract
2 1/2 cups flour
2 1/2 teaspoons baking
    powder
1 1/2 teaspoons baking soda
1/2 teaspoon salt
1 teaspoon cinnamon
2 tablespoons
    confectioners' sugar
1/2 teaspoon cinnamon

Yield: 10 servings

- Cream butter in mixer bowl until light. Add sugar gradually, beating constantly until fluffy. Add chocolate; mix well. Beat in eggs 1 at a time. Add milk, zucchini, orange rind and vanilla; mix well.
- Combine flour, baking powder, baking soda, salt and 1 teaspoon cinnamon. Add to chocolate mixture; mix well. Spoon into greased and floured 10-inch bundt pan.
- Bake at 350 degrees for 1 hour and 5 minutes or until wooden pick inserted in center comes out clean. Cool in pan for 10 to 15 minutes; remove to wire rack.
- Sift mixture of confectioners' sugar and 1/2 teaspoon cinnamon over cake. Cool completely.

Sharon West DaRe

Chocolate Shadow Cake

1 (2-layer) package
  chocolate cake mix
2 cups whipping cream
1 cup confectioners' sugar
1/2 cup baking cocoa
1/2 teaspoon almond
  extract

Yield: 12 servings

• Prepare and bake cake mix using package directions for two 8-inch cake pans. Cool in pans for 10 minutes; remove to wire rack to cool completely.
• Combine whipping cream, confectioners' sugar, cocoa and almond extract in mixer bowl; beat until soft peaks form.
• Split cake layers horizontally into halves. Spread whipped cream mixture between layers and over top of cake. Garnish with chocolate chips or chocolate curls. Store in refrigerator.

Joan Grubler

Texas Sheet Cake

2 cups flour
1 teaspoon baking soda
2 teaspoons cinnamon
1 cup butter
1 cup water
1/4 cup baking cocoa
2 cups sugar
2 eggs
1/2 cup buttermilk
1 teaspoon vanilla extract
1/2 cup butter
6 tablespoons milk
1/4 cup baking cocoa
1 (1-pound) package
  confectioners' sugar
1 cup chopped pecans
24 pecan halves

Yield: 24 servings

• Sift flour, baking soda and cinnamon together.
• Bring 1 cup butter, water and 1/4 cup cocoa to a boil in saucepan. Add flour mixture; remove from heat. Mix until smooth. Add sugar, eggs, buttermilk and vanilla; beat for 2 minutes.
• Spread in greased and floured 10x15-inch cake pan. Bake at 375 degrees for 20 minutes.
• Combine 1/2 cup butter, milk and 1/4 cup cocoa in saucepan. Cook over low heat until butter melts, stirring to mix well; do not boil. Stir in confectioners' sugar and chopped pecans.
• Spoon over hot cake. Score into servings. Place 1 pecan half in center of each serving. Cool on wire rack. Cut into squares.
• Do not substitute margarine for butter in this recipe.

Mary Yanda

Grandma's Gingerbread

1/2 cup margarine,
  softened
1 cup sugar
2 teaspoons baking soda
1 cup hot water
1 cup molasses
2 1/2 cups flour
2 eggs, beaten
1 teaspoon cinnamon
1 teaspoon ginger
Salt to taste

Yield: 15 servings

• Cream margarine and sugar in mixer bowl until light. Add mixture of baking soda dissolved in hot water; mix well. Let stand for 5 minutes.
• Add molasses, flour, eggs, cinnamon, ginger and salt; mix well. Spoon into greased and floured 9x13-inch cake pan.
• Bake at 350 degrees for 35 minutes. Serve with whipped cream or vanilla ice cream.

Janet Kropp

Oatmeal Cake

1 1/2 cups boiling water
1 cup quick-cooking oats
1/2 cup butter
1 cup sugar
1 cup packed brown sugar
2 eggs
1 1/2 cups flour
1 teaspoon baking powder
1 teaspoon baking soda
1 teaspoon vanilla extract
1 teaspoon cinnamon
1/2 teaspoon salt
1/2 cup sugar
1 cup packed brown sugar
1/2 cup evaporated milk
1/4 cup butter, softened
1/2 teaspoon vanilla extract
1 cup coconut

Yield: 12 servings

• Pour boiling water over oats in bowl; let stand for 10 minutes.
• Add 1/2 cup butter, 1 cup sugar and 1 cup brown sugar; mix well. Add eggs, flour, baking powder, baking soda, 1 teaspoon vanilla, 1 teaspoon cinnamon and salt; mix well.
• Spoon into greased 9x13-inch cake pan. Bake at 350 degrees for 30 to 35 minutes or until cake tests done.
• Combine 1/2 cup sugar, 1 cup brown sugar, evaporated milk, 1/4 cup butter and 1/2 teaspoon vanilla in bowl; mix well. Stir in coconut. Spread over warm cake. Place under broiler until browned and bubbly. Cool on wire rack.

Ellen Brafford Valentine

Mandarin Orange Cake

Easy and impressive!

1 (2-layer) package yellow
  cake mix
4 eggs
2/3 cup vegetable oil
1 (11-ounce) can
  mandarin oranges
1 (20-ounce) can crushed
  pineapple, drained
13 ounces whipped
  topping
1 (4-ounce) package
  vanilla instant pudding
  mix

Yield: 12 servings

- Combine cake mix, eggs, oil and undrained
  oranges in mixer bowl; beat for 2 minutes.
  Spoon into 3 greased and floured 8-inch
  cake pans.
- Bake at 350 degrees for 15 to 20 minutes or
  until golden brown. Cool in pans for 10
  minutes; remove to wire rack to cool
  completely.
- Fold pineapple into whipped topping in
  bowl. Sprinkle pudding mix over top; mix
  well. Spread between layers and over top of
  cake. Store in refrigerator.

Alyce B. Squibb

Poppy Seed Cake

3 cups flour
2 cups sugar
1 1/2 teaspoons baking soda
1/2 teaspoon salt
1 cup vegetable oil
4 eggs
1 (13-ounce) can
  evaporated milk
1 (10-ounce) jar poppy
  seed filling
1 cup chopped pecans

Yield: 15 servings

- Sift flour, sugar, baking soda and salt into
  bowl. Beat in oil, eggs and evaporated milk;
  mix well. Add poppy seed filling and
  pecans; beat at medium speed for 2 minutes.
- Spoon into greased and floured 9x13-inch
  cake pan. Bake at 350 degrees for 50 to 60
  minutes or until cake tests done.
- May omit pecans or substitute other nuts
  for pecans.

Kathy Parsons

Poppy Seed Cake with Orange Glaze

3 cups flour
3 eggs, beaten
1 cup plus 2 tablespoons
 vegetable oil
1 1/2 teaspoons baking
 powder
1 1/2 teaspoons each
 vanilla extract, butter
 flavoring and almond
 extract
2 1/4 cups sugar
1 1/2 cups milk
2 tablespoons poppy seeds
1 1/2 teaspoons salt
3/4 cup orange juice
3/4 cup sugar
1 teaspoon vanilla extract
1/2 teaspoon almond extract
1/2 teaspoon butter
 flavoring

Yield: 24 servings

• Combine flour, eggs, oil, baking powder,
 1 1/2 teaspoons vanilla, 1 1/2 teaspoons butter
 flavoring, 1 1/2 teaspoons almond extract,
 2 1/4 cups sugar, milk, poppy seeds and salt
 in bowl; mix well. Spoon into 2 greased
 5x9-inch loaf pans.
• Bake at 350 degrees for 1 hour or until
 loaves test done.
• Combine orange juice, 3/4 cup sugar, 1
 teaspoon vanilla, 1/2 teaspoon almond
 extract and 1/2 teaspoon butter flavoring in
 bowl; mix well. Pour over hot loaves in
 pans.

Mary W. Renner

Prune Cakes

1 1/2 cups sugar
1 cup vegetable oil
3 eggs
2 cups flour
1 teaspoon baking soda
1 teaspoon each cinnamon,
 nutmeg and allspice
1 cup buttermilk
1 teaspoon vanilla extract
1 cup chopped cooked
 prunes
1 cup walnuts
1 cup sugar
1/2 cup buttermilk
1/2 teaspoon baking soda
1 tablespoon light corn
 syrup
1/4 cup butter
1/2 teaspoon vanilla extract

Yield: 24 servings

• Blend 1 1/2 cups sugar and oil in mixer bowl.
 Beat in eggs.
• Sift flour, 1 teaspoon baking soda, cinnamon,
 nutmeg and allspice together. Add to batter
 alternately with 1 cup buttermilk, mixing well
 after each addition. Stir in 1 teaspoon vanilla,
 prunes and walnuts.
• Spoon into 2 greased and floured loaf pans.
 Bake at 325 degrees for 1 hour or until
 cakes test done.
• Combine 1 cup sugar, 1/2 cup buttermilk, 1/2
 teaspoon baking soda, corn syrup, butter
 and 1/2 teaspoon vanilla in saucepan; mix
 well. Cook to soft-ball stage. Spoon over
 hot cakes. Cool in pans on wire rack. Serve
 with whipped cream.
• May bake in 4 small loaf pans if preferred.

Shirley W. Weaver

Williamsburg Apple Pie

7 cups chopped peeled
   baking apples
1/2 cup apricot preserves
1/2 cup sugar
1 tablespoon lemon juice
1 teaspoon grated lemon
   rind
3 tablespoons flour
1/4 teaspoon cinnamon
1/4 teaspoon nutmeg
1 recipe 2-crust pie pastry
2 tablespoons margarine

Yield: 8 servings

• Combine apples, preserves, sugar, lemon
  juice, lemon rind, flour, cinnamon and
  nutmeg in bowl; mix lightly.
• Spoon into pie plate lined with 1 pricked
  pastry; dot with margarine. Top with
  remaining pastry; seal edge and cut vents.
• Bake at 375 degrees for 20 minutes. Reduce
  oven temperature to 325 degrees. Bake for
  45 to 60 minutes longer or until golden
  brown.

Diana J. Davis

Upside-Down Apple Pie

1/4 cup butter, softened
1/2 cup pecan halves
1/2 cup packed brown
   sugar
1 recipe 2-crust pie pastry
6 cups sliced peeled
   apples
1/2 cup sugar
2 tablespoons flour
1/2 teaspoon cinnamon
Nutmeg to taste

Yield: 8 servings

• Spread butter over bottom and side of
  9-inch pie plate. Arrange pecan halves
  rounded side down in butter. Sprinkle with
  brown sugar; press down gently. Place half
  the pastry over brown sugar.
• Combine apples, sugar, flour, cinnamon and
  nutmeg in bowl; mix well. Spoon into
  prepared pie plate. Top with remaining
  pastry. Trim and seal edge; cut vents.
• Bake at 400 degrees for 50 minutes. Cool on
  rack for 5 minutes. Invert onto serving plate.

Lisa Rae Sims

*The Good Children's Zoo is a 65-acre natural habitat for North
American animals. The zoo also offers the Benedum Science
Theatre and a model train display. Another
attraction is the 1 1/2-mile train ride through the zoo.*

Cheese Pie

16 ounces cream cheese
3/4 cup sugar
3 eggs
1 cup sour cream
1/2 cup sugar
1 teaspoon vanilla extract

Yield: 8 servings

• Beat cream cheese in mixer bowl until light. Add 3/4 cup sugar gradually, beating constantly until fluffy. Beat in eggs 1 at a time. Spoon into buttered 10-inch pie plate.
• Bake at 325 degrees for 50 minutes. Cool on wire rack for 20 minutes; center will fall to form crust.
• Combine sour cream, 1/2 cup sugar and vanilla in bowl; mix well. Spoon into cooled crust.
• Bake for 15 minutes longer. Cool on wire rack. Serve topped with fresh fruit.

DeAnna Lee Taylor

Chart House Mud Pie

20 chocolate wafers, crushed
1/4 cup melted butter
1 gallon coffee ice cream, softened
1 1/2 cups fudge sauce

Yield: 8 servings

• Combine wafer crumbs and butter in bowl; mix well. Press into 9-inch pie plate.
• Spread ice cream over prepared layer. Top with fudge sauce.
• Freeze for 10 hours. Garnish with whipped cream and slivered almonds.
• Place fudge sauce in freezer for a short amount of time to make spreading easier.

Roanne M. Burech

Fudge Pie

This pie is really rich.

6 tablespoons baking
  cocoa
1 cup melted margarine
2 cups sugar
1/2 cup flour
4 eggs
1 teaspoon vanilla extract
1 unbaked (9-inch or
  10-inch) pie shell

Yield: 8 servings

- Combine cocoa, margarine, sugar, flour, eggs and vanilla in mixer bowl; mix until smooth. Spoon into pie shell.
- Bake at 325 degrees for 35 to 45 minutes or until set. Cool on wire rack.

Holli Massey-Smith

Fudge Pecan Pie

3 eggs
1 cup light corn syrup
1 cup sugar
2 tablespoons margarine
1 teaspoon vanilla extract
2 teaspoons dark rum
3 ounces semisweet
  chocolate chips, melted
1 unbaked (9-inch) pie
  shell
2 cups pecan halves

Yield: 8 servings

- Beat eggs slightly in bowl. Add corn syrup, sugar, margarine, vanilla and rum; mix well.
- Combine half the egg mixture with melted chocolate in bowl; mix well. Spoon into pie shell.
- Arrange pecans halves over chocolate mixture. Spoon remaining egg mixture over pecans.
- Bake at 400 degrees for 10 minutes; reduce oven temperature to 350 degrees. Bake for 40 minutes longer or until set. Cool on wire rack.

Beth R. Weaver

Peanut Butter Pie

6 ounces cream cheese,
  softened
3/4 cup confectioners'
  sugar
1/2 cup peanut butter
2 tablespoons milk
1 envelope whipped
  topping mix
1 baked (8-inch) graham
  cracker pie shell

Yield: 8 servings

- Combine cream cheese and confectioners'
  sugar in mixer bowl; beat until light and
  fluffy. Add peanut butter and milk; mix well.
- Prepare whipped topping using package
  directions. Fold into peanut butter mixture.
- Spoon into pie shell. Chill for 5 to 6 hours.
  Garnish with peanuts and chocolate syrup.

Caryn Buch

Low-Fat Pumpkin Pie

1 cup vanilla wafer crumbs
2 tablespoons melted
  margarine
2 envelopes unflavored
  gelatin
1 cup evaporated skim
  milk
1 cup canned pumpkin
1/4 teaspoon grated orange
  rind
3/4 teaspoon pumpkin pie
  spice
2 egg whites
1/8 teaspoon salt
3/4 cup packed brown
  sugar
3/4 cup plain nonfat yogurt

Yield: 8 servings

- Mix vanilla wafer crumbs with margarine in
  bowl. Press into 9-inch pie plate sprayed
  with nonstick cooking spray.
- Soften gelatin in evaporated milk in
  saucepan for several minutes. Cook over
  low heat until gelatin dissolves, stirring
  constantly.
- Add pumpkin, orange rind and pumpkin
  pie spice; mix well. Chill until partially set.
- Beat egg whites with salt at medium speed
  in mixer bowl until soft peaks form. Add
  brown sugar gradually, beating constantly
  until stiff peaks form.
- Fold egg white mixture and yogurt into
  gelatin mixture. Spoon into prepared pie
  plate. Chill until serving time.

Jan Berardinelli

*Jamboree USA is the second oldest
live radio broadcast in the United States.*

Rhubarb Custard Pie

Rhubarb Custard Pie is an old-fashioned favorite.

3 cups flour
1/8 teaspoon baking soda
1/2 teaspoon salt
1 cup shortening
1 egg yolk
1 teaspoon vinegar
2 eggs, beaten
2 tablespoons milk
1 1/2 cups sugar
3 tablespoons flour
1 tablespoon margarine
1/4 teaspoon nutmeg
1/4 teaspoon salt
3 cups chopped rhubarb

Yield: 8 servings

- Sift 3 cups flour, baking soda and 1/2 teaspoon salt into bowl. Cut in shortening until crumbly. Combine egg yolk and vinegar in 1-cup measure. Add enough water to measure 1/2 cup. Add to crumb mixture; mix well to form dough.
- Roll dough into circle on floured surface; fit into pie plate.
- Combine 2 eggs, milk, sugar, 3 tablespoons flour, margarine, nutmeg and salt in bowl; mix well. Stir in rhubarb. Spoon into pastry-lined pie plate.
- Bake at 400 degrees for 50 to 60 minutes or until rhubarb is tender and crust is golden brown.

Marilyn Grist

Fresh Strawberry Pie

A family favorite, especially in June, when the local strawberries are at their peak.

1 1/2 cups water
1 cup sugar
1 (3-ounce) package strawberry gelatin
3 tablespoons cornstarch
1/4 teaspoon salt
1/2 cup cold water
1 quart fresh strawberries, cut into halves
1 baked (9-inch) pie shell

Yield: 8 servings

- Bring 1 1/2 cups water and sugar to a boil in saucepan. Stir in gelatin until dissolved. Stir in mixture of cornstarch, salt and 1/2 cup cold water. Cook until thickened, stirring constantly. Cool completely.
- Place strawberries in pie shell. Spoon cooled glaze over strawberries. Chill for 2 hours. Garnish servings with whipped cream.

Jan Berardinelli

Walnut Oatmeal Pie in Chocolate Crust

18 chocolate wafers,
  finely crushed
3/4 cup ground walnuts
1/4 cup unsalted
  margarine, softened
3/4 cup light corn syrup
3/4 cup packed brown
  sugar
1/2 cup milk
1/4 cup melted unsalted
  margarine
2 eggs
1 teaspoon vanilla extract
3/4 cup quick-cooking oats
1/2 cup semisweet
  chocolate chips
1/2 cup chopped walnuts

Yield: 8 servings

- Combine cookie crumbs, 3/4 cup walnuts and 1/4 cup margarine in bowl; mix well. Press mixture over bottom and side of 9-inch pie shell. Bake at 350 degrees for 7 to 8 minutes. Cool on wire rack for 10 to 15 minutes.
- Whisk corn syrup, brown sugar, milk, 1/4 cup margarine, eggs and vanilla in bowl until smooth. Stir in oats, chocolate chips and 1/2 cup walnuts. Spoon into pie shell.
- Bake at 350 degrees for 45 to 50 minutes or until set, covering edge with foil if necessary to prevent overbrowning.
- Garnish with whipped cream and additional walnuts. May serve with vanilla ice cream.

Lori Dallas

Perfect Flaky Oil Pastry

3 1/2 cups flour
1 teaspoon salt
1 cup vegetable oil
1/2 cup water

Yield: 2 pie shells

- Mix flour and salt in large bowl. Add oil and water; mix lightly with fork. Shape into 2 balls; flatten slightly.
- Roll each portion into circle between sheets of waxed paper. Fit into pie plates; fill and bake as desired.
- May store unbaked pastry in freezer for 2 months.

Brenda G. Moore

Index

WHEELING

R. R. Supper—Bill of Fare

On March 4, 1852, the McLure House hosted a grand railroad supper. Although little is known about this event, it is assumed that it was in celebration of the plans of the B & O Railroad to begin service to Wheeling within the year.

On December 24, 1852, the tracks were joined at Roseby's Rock, near Grave Creek, Marshall County.

The first train of the Baltimore and Ohio Railroad arrived in Wheeling on January 12, 1853. The banquet for one thousand included lobster salad, buffalo tongues, and capon with mushrooms. Among those in attendance were four hundred people from Baltimore, the governors of Maryland and Virginia, members of both legislatures, and local dignitaries.

photograph courtesy of the Ohio County Public Library

Index

Index

Index

Index

The Mingo Indian statue stands at the crest of Wheeling Hill as a reminder of the Native Americans who inhabited the Ohio Valley when the Zane family founded Wheeling in 1769. The statue's inscription reads: "The Mingo, original inhabitant of this valley, extends greetings and peace to all wayfarers."

The settlers and the Mingo had a friendly relationship for several years, until April 1774 when the family of Mingo

Mingo Indian

leader Tal-ga-yee-ta, also known as Logan, was massacred near Steubenville, Ohio. This massacre was the catalyst of Dunmore's War, named for the then royal governor of Virginia. This war resulted in the construction of several forts along the Ohio River, including the construction of Fort Henry, originally called Fort Fincastle, at Wheeling in July 1774. Dunmore's War and residual fighting continued periodically until 1795.

As settlers encroached more and more on the land, Native Americans began to disappear from the Ohio Valley, with few remaining by the nineteenth century. However, a number of Mingo would give archery demonstrations at festivals in Wheeling in the 1820s.

Wheeling artist Henry Jacob Beu cast the bronze statue. It was a gift to the city from the Kiwanis Club and George W. Lutz. The statue was dedicated in June 1928.

Notes

Mingo Indian